FINDING THE TRAIL OF LIFE

FINDING THE TRAIL OF LIFE

RUFUS M. JONES

GYAN

Published by

Gyan Publishing House
5, Ansari Road
Daryaganj, New Delhi-110002
Phone: 011-47034999, 9811692060
E-mail: books@gyanbooks.com

Distribution Network
gyanbooks.com
India, USA, Canada, UK, Australia

ISBN: 978-93-6280-285-9 (HB)

First Published, 1926

2nd Impression 2025

Printed at: Gyan Press, Delhi.

FINDING THE TRAIL OF LIFE
Author: RUFUS M. JONES

FINDING THE TRAIL OF LIFE

By

RUFUS M. JONES

Professor of Philosophy in Haverford College

"I have not so far left the coasts of life
To travel inland, that I cannot hear
That murmur of the outer Infinite,
Which unweaned babies smile at
in their sleep
When wondered at for smiling."
MRS. BROWNING *in Aurora Leigh.*

LONDON: GEORGE ALLEN & UNWIN, LTD.
RUSKIN HOUSE 40 MUSEUM STREET, W.C.1.

DEDICATION

To the undimmed memory of the little boy who lived by my side here on earth for eleven happy years and who showed me what an ideal and perfect childhood could be.

CONTENTS

INTRODUCTION

Some years ago I wrote a little book entitled *A Boy's Religion from Memory.* It was many times reprinted and was in its day widely read. I had the pleasure of knowing that William James loved it, and I had plenty of evidence too that boys and girls enjoyed it. Summer after summer in recent years I have been going back to my old birthplace and many memories have come to life there which were below the threshold when the little book was written a quarter of a century ago. Instead of reprinting it, therefore, as I have been asked to do, I have decided to write a new book covering a somewhat longer period of boyhood and youth. I have preserved what was quick and vital in the old narrative, but there is so much that is new and fresh, or entirely retold, that it is a new book and deserves a new title.

I do not want it to be read as an autobiography or a book of "confessions." It is written to interpret the religion of a boy and to show the boy in his struggle to get through the jungle and to find the trail of life. There is nothing ideal about the boy who figures in these pages. He was country born and bred, and there is much wild flavor apparent in him. He had all the battles to fight with temptations that any real boy is familiar with, but religion was always one of the main factors of his early drama. In this particular, I believe, the boy of this book is like the average boy. He is more concerned over his spiritual condition than he is over anything else, though nobody knows it or suspects it. He may be easily turned against religion by unwise handling, but if the atmosphere about him is right, and he finds the right group-guidance, he will come into religion as naturally as he comes into the other great inheritances of the race.

I am convinced, too, by my own life and by wide observation of children that mystical experience is much more common than is usually supposed. Children are not so absorbed as we are with things and with problems. They are not so completely organized for dealing with the outside world as we older persons are. They do not live by cut-and-dried theories. They have more room for surprise and wonder. They are more sensitive to intimations, flashes, openings. The invisible impinges on their souls and they *feel* its reality as something quite natural. Wordsworth was no doubt a rare and unusual child, but many a boy, who was never to be a poet, has felt as he did. "I was often unable," he says, in the preface to his great "Ode," "to think of external things as having external existence, and I communed with all that I saw as something not apart from, but inherent in, my own immaterial nature. Many times while going to school have I grasped at a wall or tree to recall myself from this abyss of idealism to the reality." The world within is just as real as the world without until events force us to become mainly occupied with the outside one.

Some of my readers will no doubt question my powers of memory. They will suspect that what I call memory is really imagination. It is notoriously difficult to draw a sharp line between these two processes of the mind. I know how easy it is to color a story with the hue that comes from mature experience. I will not assert that I have always spoken, as in the solemn witness box, "the whole truth and *nothing but* the truth." But I have done my honest best to tell what verily happened to me; what I saw, and felt. I have with restraint refused to beautify and adorn, or to introduce many a narrative which I felt had too much imaginative color to be hand-on-the-heart truth. I used to know an ol Friend, who was so exact in his statements that he always said, "I think, or at least I think that I think!" Once when he had sciatica he was asked how he felt and he cautiously remarked,

"I have a feeling that is akin to pain." I may not have kept as close to the underside of truth as my ancient Friend did, but what I have told is pretty near the line of real events. It can be taken quite safely as the real *experience* of the boy I myself once was—*quorum pars fui*.

These chapters will, however, be in vain if they fail to indicate how difficult is the task of discovering what goes on within the boy, or if they fail to show what delicate treatment is required to bring him through his budding periods and his shifting ideals to a clear and well-defined life purpose. If boys are better than they seem to be, as this book maintains, they are also much more difficult to understand than is generally believed, and their lives are in more unstable equilibrium. The parents' responsibility is most assuredly a solemn one, for in the days of boyhood the invisible structure of a self is silently being woven, and the social environment is a tremendous factor in the final product. Here is the modest effort to tell how one boy's life formed itself, and what the environment was.

The secondary purpose of the writer has been to preserve a little longer the memory of a form of religious life and of a set of customs which one must confess are either passing away or have already passed away. Quakerism is still a living force.

It is a present faith, and it has a great potential future. But the Quakerism which was the atmosphere of this boy's life has in a large measure already ceased from the earth. It was a unique type of religious life, and it kept its peculiar form only as long as it existed apart from the currents of the larger social whole. The movements of modern complex life have forced it either to die out or undergo transformation. It was a beautiful faith, and it produced rare types of personal sainthood whose story is not yet written. In this simple way some impressions of this spiritual atmosphere, with its local color, are caught and preserved, though it is only a thumb-nail sketch.

A little child, who had seen the wonderful cathedral windows of England with their saints in glorious color, described a saint as "a person who lets the light come through." That is just what happens. The saint lets the light come through.

> "Through such souls alone
> God stooping shows sufficient of His light
> For us in the dark to rise by."

But my "saints" not only let the light through for me in the dark to rise by, but they were also always pulling me upward and forward by invisible cords, somewhat as the moon lifts the ocean. Our many visitors used to tell me much about the tides in the Bay of Fundy, which was not so very far away from my home. It seemed amazing that the moon with no tackle and no derrick could lift all this mass of water high above the surrounding sea and then let it swirl sixty feet high into this funnel of a bay. But it is even more wonderful how somebody's life, without the attachment of string or rope, will raise a boy from low level to high and change all his goings. It is as fine a miracle as there is, and when it happens it is worth telling about.

Homer's *Odyssey* is no doubt more romantic, and is told with much more verve and marching power than falls to the lot of my simple narrative of a country boy's life. But in one point, by no means a negligible one, my story strikes a note which his misses. He portrays, with unsurpassed epic grandeur, the heroic deeds, the hazardous wanderings, the marvelous escapes and the final home-coming of a man who never grows old, who moves about the world with an immortal youth. But the ancient bard's interest terminates with his hero's *deeds*. He turns no searchlight in to reveal the inner drama of his soul. His narrative follows the paths which a man walks with his feet or covers with his boat. My story, however trivial in comparison, has to do all the time with the labyrinthine ways of the soul. The feet go somewhere in this story and so does the boat, but always the real drama is concerned with the shaping of a viewless and invisible life within a crude and half-formed body. The hero here, too, like Homer's hero, is immortal and is on a strange pilgrimage in quest of a country and a home beyond the voices and the wanderings.

FINDING THE TRAIL OF LIFE.

CHAPTER I
The Dawn of Memory

It is always worth while to see how a boy thinks about himself and about his world. The trouble is that very few boys betray their deepest thoughts and musings, and when they get old enough to tell what was going on in their inside world, they have become too old to remember the details. Their boyhood ideas get all mixed up and fused in with the maturer thoughts and reflections of the grown man, and the boy's real inner life never gets quite revealed. I hope I have not yet "traveled so far inland" that I have entirely forgotten how I fared when my world was new, and I shall try to gather up some of my experiences in that happy period when my life was still feeling the tides of the boundless sea which brought me hither.

We never remember anything about the most important years of our lives—those first three when we are really getting under way, when we learn to eat, to laugh, to walk, and to talk, when we discover that *we are* and that other persons *are* and that things which we see *are*, when we come upon the mighty fact that we have a will of our own, and that we *must* nevertheless obey Something not ourselves, Something higher than we. Nothing can be more important to us than the formation of our disposition. It means more than houses or lands, more than clothes or bank accounts, stocks or bonds. It underlies everything we think and do. It is closer to us than our blood or bones. It settles whether we shall laugh or cry, whether we shall make friends or travel a lonely path. Why do not fathers and mothers give more attention to the earliest stages of education—this fundamental education which makes us what we are going to be!

Anyway, those first three years are blank to us, they will not come back. They are like the water which the mill has used and which has gone on never to flow back upon itself. Others may tell us little snatches out of this lost strip of ourselves, and we may have heard things which we half believe that we *remember*, but few of us are sound authorities on the wisdom of those submerged years. But this much I know. I came into a world where love was waiting for me, and into a family in which religion was as important an element for life as was the air we breathed or the bread we ate.

Mine was a family woven out of the strands

of many diverse racial stocks. There was an important Celtic strain in me. Thomas Jones, my far-removed ancestor, very kindly came over from Wales to Hanover, Massachusetts in the eighteenth century. By a series of happy marriages his offspring connected me up with four colonial Governors of Rhode Island—Nicholas Easton, John Easton, John Coggeshall and Caleb Carr, and, what is still more important, linked me up with the blood and spirit that flowed from the great John Robinson of Leyden. My grandmother on my father's side was of Irish stock. She was a Jepson, which was in my boyhood always pronounced "Jipson," and her grandfather was Erin born—"Erigena." My mother was a Hoxie and her mother was a Goddard.

Going back far enough, the Hoxie strain had a French origin, though for many centuries it was good English stock. Among its good traits it had a wholesome appreciation of humor and love of it. All these ancestral lines took naturally to the Quaker faith and my roots for many generations were deep down in Quaker subsoil.

There were, however, in spite of my favorable inheritance, some features connected with my arrival which might naturally discourage a newcomer. The house to which I came was most plainly furnished; it was a good many miles from any city; a cold, bleak winter was at its height—January 25th—and there seemed to be almost no conveniences for comfort and few preparations for what we usually call culture. But these matters troubled me not a bit. It never occurred to me that this was a world of inequalities and I had no prevision of the struggle by which one wins what he gets.

The only real fact I can relate about these first hours is one which shows what the highest ambition of my family was and it will also illustrate a characteristic trait in the member of my family who did very much to shape my life in those years when I was plastic to the touch. As soon as I came into the arms of my Aunt Peace, my father's oldest sister who lived with us—one of God's saints—she had an "opening" such as often came to her, for she was gifted with prophetic vision. "This child," she said, "will one day bear the message of the Gospel to distant lands and to peoples across the sea." It was spoken solemnly and with a calm assurance as though she saw the little thing suddenly rising out of her lap to go. That prophecy may seem like a simple word but it expressed the highest ideal of that devoted woman, and her faith in the fulfillment never slackened, even when the growing boy showed signs of doing anything else rather than realizing that hope. If the neighbors, in the period of my youth, had been told of this prophecy it would, I am afraid, almost have shaken their faith in the forevision of this remarkable woman whom they all loved and whose insight they implicitly trusted.

While I was too young to have any religion of my own, I had come to a home where religion kept its fires always burning. We had very few "things," but we were rich in invisible wealth. I was not "christened" in a church, but I was sprinkled from morning till night with the dew of religion. We never ate a meal which did not begin with a hush of thanksgiving; we never began a day without "a family gathering" at which mother read a chapter of the Bible, after which there would follow a weighty silence. These silences, during which all the children of our family were hushed with a kind of awe, were very important features of my spiritual development. There was work inside and outside the house waiting to be done, and yet we sat there hushed and quiet, doing nothing. I very quickly discovered that something *real* was taking place. We were feeling our way down to that place from which living words come and very often they did come. Some one would bow and talk with God so simply and quietly that He never seemed far away. The words helped to explain the silence. We were now finding what we had been searching for. When I first began to think of God I did not think of Him as very far off. At meeting some of the Friends who prayed shouted loud and strong when they called upon Him, but at home He always heard easily and He seemed to be there with us in the living silence. My first steps in religion were thus *acted*. It was a religion which we *did* together. Almost nothing was *said* in the way of instructing me. We all joined together to listen for God and then one of us talked to Him for the others. In these simple ways my religious disposition was being unconsciously formed and the roots of my faith in unseen realities were reaching down far below my crude and childish surface thinking.

The first event of my life which I truly remember is a visit to the house of our nearest and best loved neighbor. I wandered off alone hoping no doubt to find there as a playmate a little boy who was a few months younger than myself. On this occasion no one was at home but the door was open and I walked in and surveyed the scene. The little boy's mother, a woman of many gifts, had among her carefully tended plants a rare and wonderful fuchsia in full bloom. I can see it now with its brightly colored, long hanging flowers. I went up to it with a kind of wild fascination and picked off every one of the flowers. Then I began to feel that all was not well with me. Something inside smote me. I felt confused and uncomfortable. I couldn't put them on again, and so the next best thing to do seemed to be to hide them. I carried them out and put them one by one down the wide cracks in the steps leading up to the porch. I was just finishing my neat job of concealing the fuchsias when our neighbors—the father, mother and little boy—drove into the yard. I had the last red blossom in my hand as the mother came up to the step. She went into the house and viewed the havoc and desolation and then returned to tell me what she thought of me as a visitor! Sufficient to say I went home with a very low opinion of myself. What the outraged neighbor said only confirmed what I had already begun to feel inside myself. It is not an accident that this is my first memory. It is precisely the moment when my self-consciousness was born. I here suddenly discovered something in myself I could not altogether control or manage. Something confronted me, reproved me and made me ashamed; something in me *hurt* me as much as the neighbor's stern words did.

The next story I remember out of this dim period of my youth shows how religion filtered into my play. Our house was one of the headquarters of traveling Quaker ministers, of whom I shall have more to say later, and my father used to drive through the community to "appoint" meetings for them. I was always hearing about "'pointed meetings," whatever they might be. So when the little tots came to play with me, I worked out my budding Quakerism on them. I gathered them in a row on the floor and told them to sit still, for we were going to have "'pointed meeting." Then I stood up in front and *pointed* with great solemnity at each one of them.

I began to go to school the summer after my fourth birthday. The little rustic, but not red, schoolhouse was half a mile from our house. I walked back and forth with my little sister who was four years older than myself. School began at nine o'clock in the morning, closed at twelve; began again at one and closed for the day at four. We had a fifteen minute recess of happy memory in the middle of the forenoon and again in the middle of the afternoon. School opened in the morning with a chapter of the Bible, followed sometimes with silence, and sometimes, when the teacher had a gift for it, with vocal prayer. I always thought of education, in my early days, as religious business and it never occurred to me that you could have a real school without reading the Bible in it.

It was a long day for a four-year-old boy whose feet did not yet reach the floor, for there was so little to do and no interesting way to fill up the time in between the "sessions" of the primer class.

Everything about the school was old fashioned. None of our teachers ever heard of Froebel or Pestalozzi and the word "pedagogy" would have meant no more to any of them than did "that blessed word Mesopotamia." The first step on the long journey to truth was learning to "say" the alphabet, then learning to recognize the same letters when put together in words. This was a monotonous and tedious task and I feel a good deal of sympathy with the little boy who under similar circumstances was told to "say A." He hesitated and then said, "I'm not going to say A, for if I say A, you'll want me to go on and say B."

I soon got interested in watching and listening to the classes which met on the benches close in front of me, for everything happened in the one room where we all sat. I listened to the reading lessons. I saw the black board and I was full of interest watching the teacher correct and punish the unruly or the too playful children. Here I got my first ideas about moral discipline. There were prizes for those who did well and forceful restraints or disagreeable consequences for those who wasted their time or who disobeyed the teacher's rules. This little social world which made our school was a difficult one to manage and govern. We were of many ages. We had a great variety of homes and home training. We were all thrown together in a single room, with two children sitting together in a seat. Classes were reciting in front while the rest were studying. It was a cross-section of our larger democratic life, where each one has his own bent of life, but where all must somehow get on together. I got my alphabet that first year, but I got a great many other things, both good and bad with it. The one episode I remember the most vividly out of the blur and confusion of that first year of my public education is a case of threatened punishment. Our teacher sometimes indulged in over-vigorous "terrorizing" of her little folks and on this occasion she told one of "the babes and sucklings" in our primer class that if he ever repeated what he had just done she would "tie a string around his neck and hang him up on a nail above her desk and let his legs dangle." I really thought she would do it. I was terribly frightened, but also half fascinated with the mental picture of this squirming, wiggling boy dangling from a nail.

Whenever I go back to the headwaters of my stream of life I always see my "Grandmother Susie" sitting in the rocking chair by the open fire. She was a Jepson and gave me my Irish strain. She was born just as the Revolutionary War was ending, so that her life and mine together spanned the entire history of the United States! She was a tiny girl when the great Constitution of our nation was framed, and she stayed with us until I was fourteen. She lived under every President from George Washington to Rutherford B. Hayes. She was full of lore and wisdom. She knew an abundance of stories of the olden times. She had seen real forest Indians and had had wild bears of the woods for neighbors. Catamounts and wild-cats were more than words to her—she had seen them in the trees of the cow-pasture. She was better than a dozen story books. She could say, "I saw." Instead of beginning with the words "once upon a time," she would begin by saying, "When we were crossing the lake on the ice one winter we saw . . ." My! It was all thrilling and it was a great stimulus to imagination and wonder. What a dav it was when "Aunt Lois," grandmother's sister, came to spend the day and the two old ladies started off on their endless trails of reminiscence. They both belonged to the old school of frontier nobility and consequently they smoked long clay pipes. It never occurred to me that old women should not smoke. I supposed that it was a mark of distinction. If anybody had the odor of sanctity about her it was grandmother, and I thought of her smoke as fitting incense. She was neat and refined, and for half her long life she had been an "Elder" in the Society of Friends. Her religion had gone all through her fiber; her faith emerged in practice, and (except for her use of tobacco) she had no blemishes, and I did not think of this as a blemish. I thought she was perfect and I adored her. She had brought up eleven children and she had preserved a touch of wisdom to bestow upon a grandson. I still rank her among the glories and sublimities which surrounded my childhood. She reached back in the long stretches of her life to the mystic time when God talked with people, and I assumed that she knew Him in a different way from us who were later born, and I listened to her in reverence and joy. She helped to create our home atmosphere, and she added her gleam of light to the general spiritual radiance of that early dawn.

One of the earliest home memories out of the dim period of "first years" is the return of my Aunt Peace—the aunt of the prophecy—from an extensive religious visit through the Quaker meetings of Ohio and Iowa. I was, of course, most impressed with the things she brought me. They were as wonderful to me as the dark-skinned natives, which Columbus carried back, were to the people who crowded about his returning ship. Iowa was farther off then than the Philippines are now. But the next impression was made by the marvelous stories of special providences and strange leadings which had been experienced on the journey. I listened as though one of the Argonauts was telling of his adventures in search of the golden fleece. Every place where there was a Quaker meeting-house had its peculiar episode which I had told over and over to me. Every little boy whom she had seen and talked with in that far-flung world was described to me and called by name. This was the first event which made me realize that the world was so big. Before this, it seemed to me that it came to an end where the sky touched the hills. But now my aunt had been out beyond the place where the sky came down, and she had found the earth still going on out there! But after all, the most wonderful thing was the way in which God took care of her and told her what to do and to say in every place where she went. It seemed exactly like the things they read to me out of the life of Joseph and Samuel and David, and I supposed that everybody who was good had their lives cared for and guided in this wonderful way. I made up my mind to be good and to be one of the guided kind!

But I got a sad awakening which disturbed me and made me discover a fact which puzzles old heads as well as young ones—the fact that the righteous sometimes *suffer*. One night the Baptist Church—the only church building in our little village—burned to the ground. The neighbors suspected that it was set on fire and they appointed a committee to find out who did it. They soon found that it was part of a deep-laid scheme of revenge. In our village one man sold liquor, though it was against the law of Maine to do so. He was a very hard and dangerous man. I was always afraid of him, as though he ate little boys. Well, a temperance meeting had been held in this church which stirred the community to action and this liquor-seller had been convicted and fined. My father had been one of the leaders in bringing him to justice. The liquor-seller paid his fine and then laid his plans to "get even" with those who had interfered with his business. He hired a poor, feeble-minded man to burn the church where the speeches were made and he planned next if he hadn't been caught, to burn our house. Fortunately, our house did not get burned, but I got a shock from the threatened danger. It seemed then that it was risky to be good! You might get your house burned if you tried to stop bad men from being bad. Out of it all I got some little glimpse into the nature of the world, and, though I could not yet solve the problem of evil, I began to think about it!

CHAPTER II

IN A WORLD OF LOVE AND FEAR

I cannot remember when I did not think about God and wonder about Him. It was hard to make my different ideas of Him fit together. I supposed that He lived in a beautiful city—above the blue dome of the sky, which always appeared to be exactly over the top of our house where the highest place in the sky surely was. But then, too, He was everywhere else. He made the flowers bloom. He made the grass grow. He guided the birds in their flight. He made the sheen and glory on our lake at sunset. He brought me a little brother when I was four years old. He was near enough to hear good persons talk to Him when they prayed. He could see every bad thing I did. When we had "silence" after "morning reading" I always thought He was somewhere near, telling mother or Aunt Peace what to pray for and then hearing them when they spoke. They often asked Him to make me a good boy and I gradually came to believe that He was always looking after me. I ought to have been courageous and free from fear. I was surrounded with love, both on earth and in heaven, and I ought to have had a triumphant sense that all was safe and right.

The difficulty is that a boy's life is not all the time steered and controlled by reason. He is not a rationally contrived machine that always does what you expect it to do. There are many unexpected happenings and constant surprises. There are regions in him which no one explores and about which he knows as little as outside observers do. Rationality is only one of the many factors that make up a boy's life. Instincts, emotions and moods are mighty things and they have their innings as well as the intellect does—in fact, they get their turn at the bat even oftener. With all my "reasons" for being calm and fearless, I was a child full of fanciful fears. I was especially afraid of three things—of the dark, of lightning and of death. I feel sure now, as I look back on this period that I must have had some great shock of fright in that early time before I had any conscious memory of it. My fears were sometimes overpowering, and they often swept over me when there was no good reason for them. I eventually got entirely free of them and I am speaking about them here because I have no doubt that many other children have unnecessary fears as I did. It may help them to hear how I got over mine.

As previously mentioned, I was dreadfully afraid of the dark. I thought it was "inhabited." It seemed to me as though some kind of "beings" were in it. Nobody ever told me anything about this—it all came from my own imagination. The cellar where we kept our year's stock of apples and all our winter vegetables was terribly dark. When I went for apples I always carried a lamp, but there was a compartment of the cellar unfortunately near the apple-bin, which was partitioned off and absolutely dark. I always felt that "something" might come out of there any minute and "get me." I leaned away from it and was always braced ready to run to safety if anything happened. I never went down to the cellar without talking in a loud voice, or singing, and I indicated by my conversation that I had strong helpers above stairs. But when I reached the top of the stairs on my return to light and civilization, I always felt as though I had had an "escape" from pretty certain danger. A few years ago I had a strange confirmation of how deep-seated these early fears must have been. I went into that old dark compartment of the cellar, when I was on a visit to the early home, to look for something. All of a sudden, I found my body trembling like an aspen leaf. My mind was calm and unafraid but a subterranean memory had for an instant swept in on me and possessed my body with a fear which my mind did not in the least share!

There was another place worse than the cellar, and that was an attic which opened out from my bedroom. It was a most "risky" place in which to sleep. I fastened the door to this attic the moment I got to my room, if it was not already fastened, but I never felt completely safe in that direction. My terrifying dreams all through my life have been linked up with that attic. I still dream that I hear footsteps outside and then I hear a heavy thumb laid on a door-latch which goes up and down as though the door were about to open. I awake frightened to find that there is a knob on my door now and that this latch which I saw in my dream was the door-latch of my ancient attic. My dream taps that old submerged region in me where my fears used to hold sway.

Many children are naturally afraid of lightning and it is not strange that I stood in awe of it. Our thunder showers were unusually severe. Our house stood on a hill as a kind of target for bolts and the neighborhood registered some bad "hits." Once in the middle of the winter, on one of the coldest days of the year, a freak thunder storm broke over our village and a nearby house was struck and burned to the ground, and a woman living in it, who was one of mother's friends, died of heart failure from fright. This event burned a deep impression into my sensitive soul. When summer came, I watched the thunderheads with ominous dread. I kept asking father, who was a weather expert, whether he supposed we were "going to get a shower to-day." Then, as the great black cloud formed in the western sky, I got nervous and worried. There was always a "chance" that it might go north, around the lake into Albion, or possibly south to devastate Windsor. I felt little concern for these near-lying territories. In fact, I sometimes breathed a swift prayer that the threatening shower might "go 'round," particularly as Windsor was a "Democratic" town while ours was righteously "Republican." I learned one day at school that if you had a chair with glass legs and sat without touching the floor with your feet, lightning was powerless to hit you. How I longed for such a chair! There was a theory afloat that one was pretty safe on a feather-bed, as lightning couldn't go through feathers. After hearing that, I preferred showers at night, for I slept, like all country boys, on a feather-bed.

One other fear ruled me. It was the fear of death. One of my dearest playmates died while he was only a little boy, which warned me that it was not alone old people who were summoned to go. Mother went one day to the funeral of one of her lifelong friends, and when she came home there was a spot on the ribbon that tied her bonnet. I asked her what caused the spot, and she told me that it was caused by a tear that dropped from her cheek at the grave. I can still *see* that spot, across all the years. I was always asking questions about death, questions nobody could answer. Two or three times, while still very small, I had very narrow escapes, in moments of unexpected peril. I fell once head foremost into a small hole in the hay-mow, and almost smothered to death in the thick hay. I thought I was dying and made frantic efforts to "back out" of my stifling prison, but the place was so tight I could not extricate myself. My playmates were there and could easily have saved me, but they were laughing wildly at the strange and funny movements I was making with my legs in the air, and, of course, they had no idea of the danger. At length, just in the nick of time, I gave a superhuman push and came out all black in the face. Another time, a horse ran away with me when there was no one to help me and I looked death in the face again. I played the right part in a crisis when one came; my trouble was thinking, wondering, supposing, imagining.

Everybody, everywhere I went, told "scary" stories and frightened me with what *might* happen to a boy. The climax came one evening while

I was waiting in the post office for the mail to come. Some loafers who were sitting there waiting for mail that never came, began telling of "warnings" which often came to persons just before they died. One man said, and I listened breathlessly, that you often saw mysterious lights in the road, or in your room, and that was a sure "sign" that you would soon die. He told how a friend of his was driving home in the dark, late one night, and as he went to turn in to his door-yard he saw two strange lights burning like candles each side of the road. After he got out of his wagon he went back to look at the lights but they were gone. A few days later the man died. I went home that night badly scared and for some days I dwelt upon that tale with a morbid fascination. A short time after this, I awoke in the night and saw a light burning about three or four feet from the ceiling of my room. There was nothing there to burn. It could not possibly be a "regular" light, it must be a "warning" light. I covered my head up under the clothes and felt terrified. Then I looked again and there it was burning on, though there was nothing there to burn. Then I did the most heroic act of my life. I got up, drew a chair under the mysterious light, got up in the chair, and grasped at the light with my hand. I caught hold of a long ear of seed-corn which I found afterwards that father had hung up in my room the day before. A beam of the moon through a hole in my curtain had struck the ear of corn and made my terrifying "light." I went back to bed a "new" boy. I was never again afraid of "mysterious lights." I had taken a momentous step toward freedom from foolish fears.

The thing which had the most to do, however, with my deliverance from fear was my childlike discovery that God was with me and that *I belonged to Him.* I say "discovery," but it was a discovery slowly made and in the main gathered from the atmosphere of our home. God, as I have said, was as *real* to everybody in our family as was our house or our farm. I soon realized that Aunt Peace *knew* Him and that grandmother had lived more than eighty years in intimate relation with Him. I caught their simple faith and soon had one of my own. I gradually came to feel assured that whatever might be there in the dark of my bedroom, God anyhow was certainly there, stronger than everything else combined. I learned to whisper to Him as soon as I got into bed—I never learned to pray kneeling by the bedside. I never saw anybody do that until I went away to boarding school. I "committed" everything to Him. I told Him that I couldn't take care of myself and asked Him to guard and keep the little boy who needed him. And then, I believed that He *would do it.* I knew that Aunt Peace never doubted and I tried to follow her plan of life. There were times in my childhood when the God I loved was more real than the things I feared and I am convinced that all children would be genuinely religious if they had someone to lead them rightly to God, to whom they belong.

There were two events that seemed to come out of the dark, which had far-reaching effects on my life. The first one was the burning of our beautiful village when I was nine years old. Twenty-two buildings, constituting practically the entire village, were wiped out in a night. It was a sublime but terrible sight, and one which I can never forget. The wind was blowing briskly and, of course, it increased in power as the fire area enlarged. I can still see the flames roll in enormous waves up over the roofs of the stores and the big houses. Our own house was just on the edge of the village and we watched in great anxiety to see whether the fire would come as far as our home, but it was stopped before it reached us. The havoc to the village was irreparable. Our splendid avenue of elms was ruined and few of the burned buildings were replaced. The fire marked a "great divide" in the life of the little town. It was never again to be the center of activity and prosperity that it had been in earlier years. I felt as I walked the roads and gazed at the desolate cellars with their smoldering embers that something had gone out of my life. For days there was an odd strange feeling in my breast. I could not shout and laugh or whistle. Something that belonged to me and contributed to my life had vanished. I saw suddenly how uncertain, how transitory, everything was, how in a few minutes what had been so important and so precious ceased to be at all. We all knew, too, that a wicked man had done all this and had brought this disaster to pass, so that I came to realize at this early period that the world is a checkerboard place with black squares on it as well as white squares.

The day before our "great fire" I had discovered a source of vast future wealth and had entered upon a commercial enterprise which promised an independent fortune. The man in whose store the fire originated had promised me five cents a pound for all the wintergreen leaves I would pick or get other boys to pick. I spent one day in this lucrative business and was getting ready to organize the boy-force of our village to comb all the pastures for these fragrant leaves, when suddenly in an immense puff of flames the enterprise came to an instant terminus and all my hopes of wealth vanished over night. I found a poor substitute to this get-rich-quick scheme by picking nails in the cellars of the burnt area and selling them for a cent a pound. They were much heavier than the wintergreen leaves and it did not take long to pile up a pound and register a cent, but the supply was soon exhausted and this commercial operation came to an end before anything like a fortune had been accumulated. Another ambitious scheme of mine fell through. It was a plan to organize the boys into a business firm and to dig up the old empty cellars and sell them out in small pieces to the farmers for post-holes! This fine scheme broke down because of an inherent and baffling difficulty in the very nature of space itself. We discovered that you cannot parcel space out and transmit sections of it over into other spaces because these other spaces are already space. And thus while my attractive business plan and venture led to no pot of gold, it helped me to find one of the most interesting mysteries of space and to experience a new way of wonder—which is the next best thing to solving a problem.

The other event was far more personal and intimate. The next summer, when I was ten years old, I passed through a serious illness which profoundly changed my outlook on life. It began with a slight bruise on my foot, the kind to which no country boys pay much attention. I let it go until I had a deep infection. The doctor came, a kindly man, who had helped to bring me into the world, but who knew not a thing about antiseptic surgery. He sharpened his lancet on a scythe stone from the barn and then thrust it into my foot. His intention was well meant but he loaded my foot with a new infection which brought me very close to death's doors. I lost a whole year of school and in the long period of pain and fear I was brought face to face with issues of life and death which most small boys escape. It greatly deepened my religious feelings and it awoke in a wonderful way my consciousness of my mother's love. Nothing in my life ever did more to open the door between the unseen and the seen than did this long illness in my tenth year. There is a much overworked theory which connects the birth of religion with adolescence. Many things, both good and bad in us, which are usually linked up with the crisis of adolescence have been in evidence long before that somewhat artificial date is reached; and there can, I think, be no question that the deepest fact of the child's religion is his conviction, however got, of an unseen world impinging on his world of things. It shows itself in a great variety of ways in different children—much more in some than in others —and while in a multitude of children it does not rise to the level of a conscious outlook, many actions and reflections reveal that it *operates* all the same as an urge or a driving force. The healthy child is so much occupied with "things," is so busy with games and ways of motion, speed, and transit through space, that he is apt to "mask" his interest in any other kind of world. As Robert Browning puts it:

> "The child
> Feels God a moment, ichors o'er the place,
> Plays on and grows to be a man like us."

But many things occur, or may occur, in the child's life which throw him back on his deeper intimations. He may for a long time preserve that sensitive spot in him unscarred, "unichored." He may find his outside world more or less spoiled and then he may turn a good deal more than he otherwise would have done toward the world he *feels* but cannot touch. When the powers of normal activity break down and the threshold between the seen and the unseen wears thin the eternal becomes almost or quite as real as the here and now. The Beyond *gets through* much better in some states and conditions than it does in others, and I seem to have come, without knowing it, to one of these favorable junctions. Anyhow, there were many times in those long months out of school and away from playmates when a circuit seemed to close and I had some sort of contact with a larger Life. I woke up one morning wondering whether I should ever get well again and rather inclined to the negative conclusion. I dimly felt that I was slowly going from bad to worse and that there was no earthly future for me. When the time came to dress my foot that morning a piece of bone was seen coming through the opening in it. I felt sure that this was the beginning of the end. I was plainly breaking up and going to pieces! What hope could there be when my bones were coming out! I broke down and wept with all the sense of tragedy that breaks over a child's sky. At this crisis, Aunt Peace came in with her oil and balm. She could not deny that the bone was coming out, for there it was, and she did not question that I was passing through a dark tunnel in my little journey here on earth, but she insisted that it was only a "tunnel," and that I would soon emerge into the light and joy of life again. And then with her prophetess face all lighted up with the warmth and glow of her vision, she said: "This is not the end; this is the beginning. There are much better things ahead than behind. God is going to make thy coming days thy best days." My fear vanished, my discouragement disappeared. I was ready to live again. In her faith, I found my own. If God had written those words across the sky I should not have believed them any more implicitly, or been more certain that they were from Him, than I was as I listened to her and saw her unforgettable face all radiant there in my dim room. God, I felt sure, was not far away beyond the world. He was there talking to me through a person who, I well knew, belonged to Him and spoke for Him.

Not only did the unseen world become very real to me during these months of illness, but I got also during these same months a conviction, which I have never lost, that the moral laws of God execute themselves everywhere in the universe, just as the laws of gravitation do. I began to be as afraid of doing mean, wrong things when I was alone as when people were watching me. Somebody told me that Nod where Cain went after he killed Abel, meant "the land of trembling." That derivation is probably unsound, but anyhow it was true to the facts of my experience. I found that I trembled and was afraid when I did wrong, even when I did not get caught, and that feeling took all the fun out of the deed. I did not enjoy living with myself after I had done certain things! I found that I had to go to bed in a dark room and sleep with the boy who had done *that!* In a way I discovered for myself what Emerson and Carlyle at this very time were preaching so loudly, though I had never seen their names or heard their words. I knew already that one of the heaviest words in our human language was: Thou *must*.

I said "thee" and "thy" to everybody, and I would fully as soon have used profane words as have said "you" or "yours" to any person. I thought only "Friends" went to heaven, and so I supposed that the use of "thee" and "thy" was one of the main things which determined whether one would be let in or not. Nobody ever told me anything like this, and if I had asked anybody at home about it, I should have had my views corrected. But for a number of years this was my settled faith. I pitied the poor neighbors who would never be let in, and I wondered why everybody did not "join the meeting" and learn to say "thee" and "thy." I had one little Gentile friend whom I could not bear to have "lost," and I went faithfully to work and taught him "the language," which he always used with me until he was ten or twelve years old, when the strain of the world got too heavy upon the little fellow!

I am quite sure no Israelite in the days of Israel's prosperity ever had a more certain conviction that he belonged to a peculiar people whom the Lord had chosen as His own, than I did. There was for me an absolute break between "us" and anybody else. This phariseeism was never taught me or encouraged directly by anybody, but I none the less had it. If I had anything in the world to glory over it was that I was a Quaker. Others about me had a good deal more that was tangible than I had. Their life was easier, and they did not have as hard a struggle to get things which they wanted as we did. But they were not "chosen" and we were! As far back as I can travel in my memory I find this sense of superiority—a sort of birthright into divine grace and favor. I think it came partly from impressions I got from traveling Friends, whose visits had an indescribable influence upon me, as I shall show later. It will, of course, seem to have been a very narrow view, and so it was, but its influence on me was decidedly important. It gave somewhat of a dignity to my little life to feel that I belonged to God's people, that out of all the world WE had been selected to be His, and that His wonders had been worked for US, and that we were objects of His special love and care.

Everybody at home, as well as many of our visitors, believed implicitly in immediate divine guidance. Those who went out from our meeting to do extended religious service—and there were many such visits undertaken—always seemed as directly selected for these momentous missions as were the prophets of an earlier time. As far back as I can remember, I can see Friends sitting talking with my grandmother of some "concern" which was heavy upon them, and the whole matter seemed as important as though they had been called by an earthly king to carry on the affairs of an empire. It was partly these cases of divine selection and the constant impression that God was using these persons whom I knew to be His messengers that made me so sure of the fact that we were His chosen people. At any rate I grew up with this idea firmly fixed, and the events which will be told in a later chapter deepened the feeling.

CHAPTER III

THE INFLUENCE OF NATURE

A boy is very much safer morally and spiritually if he has a passion for beautiful things, for beauty in nature. It is, of course, true that many persons who have possessed great aesthetic gifts and genius have not been robustly moral and it may well be granted that aesthetic appreciation does not *necessarily* discipline the will or stabilize the character. At the same time, love of beauty does tend to elevate and ennoble the soul, and it is an immense asset in the formative stage of a youth. A country boy has many chances to become crude and rough, and the influences that may carry him into coarseness crowd about him. Consequently, it is a rare blessing when he can store up opposing forces which will work silently and unconsciously on the side of the angels. That good fortune was mine. From some ancestral strain, or from some higher source, there was within me a strong native love of beauty and of what was fine. It had at first almost no guidance or specific culture, but I thrilled when I saw something that was exactly as it ought to be. The lake in front of our house was the object of beauty which first moved me. If this glorious lake had not been there my earthly story would have been a very different one. I am writing now with the same lake in front of me, and it moves me with an ever increasing spell. The important thing, however, is that primal pull upward which it gave me. The sunset colors on it are entirely beyond description. One who sits on the eastern shore, where we fortunately lived, could see the extraordinary sheen flash across the water as the sun wrapped itself with multicolored clouds in the far west. The lake was never twice alike. Through all the seasons of the year, not least in winter, and through all the hours of the day, it had its peculiar beauties.

The brook that ran into it, a quarter of a mile away, was a never-ending delight, with its ripples, its cascades and rapids, its dark pools under the bridge, its fringe of shrubs and flowers along the banks, and the mystery of its origin, far away in the woods. How could a boy grow up without a brook like that! There were no mountains near enough to be a constant inspiration and moving force. But on clear days, when the wind came out of the northwest, the mountains of western Maine formed a glorious ridge of purple on our far horizon. Mount Blue was the noblest peak, with

Saddleback and Bigelow not far behind their leader. I loved to gaze upon these venerable mountains, whose color at sunset, and especially in the winter landscape, added another glory to our earth and sky. A few miles east of us was Deer Hill, from which we could see twelve of the sixteen counties of our State, and here on fine days we could see not only "my" mountains, but also the towering summits of Mount Washington and Mount Katahdin and many other majestic headlands near and far.

One of the great experiences, memory tells me, of those early years was going to Augusta, or "to the River," as we called it. We always had a load of produce to carry down to sell and we came back loaded with supplies for the house or the farm. It was a long twelve miles over a clay road with a series of long hills each way, for the early road makers never allowed a hill to escape them. We had only hard-worked farm horses and they never overpassed the speed-limit of that period. My father was a magic driver. He could get a horse to go a little faster than anybody else I ever knew. But even so it was an all day affair, going down and coming back and seeing the town. We carried a bag of hav which the old horse munched while we ate our sandwiches and saw the sights.

There was the black Kennebec with its line of

floating logs going over the dam and under the covered bridge, which announced a fine of five dollars for driving faster than a walk. There was the majestic statehouse to see, the arsenal, the court-house, the home of James G. Blaine who was then alive in the flesh and often walked the streets. There was the long business street with buildings all of stone, so different from our country wooden ones. Then if you happened to be there at the right time of day for it, you could see a train of cars come in, as a wonder of wonders. How unspoiled I was by the rush and whirl of life! A day in Augusta was as thrilling as a journey to Paris or London would be now. Everything was novel and strange, and gave enough to think about and wonder about for months of retrospect. On one of these trips I ate my first banana—not to be compared, I thought, with a good Maine apple—and here I saw for the first time how different was the life of a boy who grew up in city streets and a city house, from that of one who had the wide world of lake and fields and woods around him. I did not envy the city boys; I pitied them. I always came back over the winding, wooded hills giving thanks in my heart that God had planted me in His wide open spaces and not in a great metropolis like Augusta, then a city of ten thousand people!

Then there were the wild flowers. I put the

water lilies first in my ranking order. The best of it was that you had to go out on the lake to get them, and there they floated. The long stem seemed to connect the lily with the mud of the bottom, but it always looked as though it were composed of diviner stuff. The next best thing the lake had to show in the way of flowers was the rue, which had leaves that gleamed like silver when we put it under the water. In fact, we always called it "silver," and never "rue." I did not know its poetic name until much later. It should be said that I knew no botany as a boy. I wish our teacher had spent less time instructing me in the geography of Russia and Terra del Fuego, and had taken a little time to give me some specific knowledge about the flowers and the birds of our own region. As it was, I grew up in absolute ignorance, as far as technical knowledge went, of the common things which a prodigal nature spread everywhere about me. Fortunately, my ignorance did not prevent me from loving and enjoying the things I could not name. "Mayflower" was a name which for me covered arbutus, anemone, hepatica and bloodroot. The first day of May meant a trip to our "back woods," where all these precious "mayflowers" abounded. It was a day of joy and wonder, and in the evening my sister and I hung may-baskets filled with these flowers at the homes of our little friends. Our woods, too, abounded with painted trillium, ladies' slipper, Indian pipe, twin flower, Solomon's seal and a great array of beautiful mosses and ferns. It was an awe inspiring and thrilling place for excursions.

The birds of our region were very numerous. The most exciting bird event was the semi-annual "honk, honk" of the far-traveling flock of wild geese who some times favored us with a peaceful night visit in our lake. They, again, like the brook, suggested mystery. They came from the far north; they flew to lands of which we had no word, and they seemed to be steered in their V-formation flight by some invisible Power. We had our pair of fine old bald eagles who had been here on the shores of the lake undisturbed when the Indians lived in these forests, and when they cut the strange figure of a human heart on the great rock opposite our shore. There was always a pair of loons nearby, and I cannot remember when I did not love to hear their weird call to each other at night, which we always believed foretokened rain! Another tradition which we held to be infallible was that nobody could ever shoot a loon. It was maintained that a bullet could not pierce the thick feathers of their bodies, and they always "dodged" a bullet which was coming at their heads! What a poor world it would be to live in that had no loons!

But the real glory of our world was the bobolink. I have seen and heard skylarks and nightingales, but I still vote for the bobolink. Their color beautifully fits their song. They are just the right size for that amazing "brook of laughter," which pours from their throats. Their season with us was short; they came from some unknown somewhere and they hatched their young in our fields, and they went back with the new brood to that mysterious somewhere, but while they were here with us they raised life to a new pitch and gave it a peculiar touch of glory. The outstanding feature of the bobolink is his magnificent enthusiasm. He is a radiant bird. I never could see how any creature *could be* as happy as he seemed to be. There were no limits or restraints to the bubbling joy which rippled forth as he teetered on a spear of "timothy" hay, or as he flashed from resting-place to resting-place like an animated bunch of melody. I should have missed something essential to the fulness of life if the bobolink had not nested in our fields.

In the winter we had in our forests the brave chickadees, the blue jay and the beautiful wood grouse, which we called "partridge". I began my trips to the woods in winter very early in life, going with father at first to ride on the sled loads of fire wood; then as soon as I could handle a small ax, I trimmed off the branches of the big trees which he felled, and I rapidly reached the stage when I could join in the splendid work of bringing the trees down. I still pride myself on being a skilled wood chopper with some of the craft of the expert woodsman. Here in the winter woods of Maine was beauty enough to feed any young soul and mine was full of joy over it.

The stars, also, filled me with awe and wonder. Our pure northern air, with its transparent quality and its high degree of visibility gave the stars a glory which they seldom have where the per cent of humidity is greater. Our "Farmers Almanac", which was almost as much used as the family Bible was, gave us successively the names of the brilliant morning and evening "stars", and I soon knew some of the great constellations. My Uncle Eli, of whom much will be said later, took me out at night as a very little boy and showed me "the Dipper" with its two pointers, which locate the North Star. The great words of Job soon set me searching for Orion and the Pleiades and Arcturus, so that I had an immense world of interest and admiration above my head as well as by the lake and in the woods. At least once each winter we had the aurora borealis in our northern sky and no boy could see that phenomenon unmoved.

I am glad to say, though I say it very humbly,

I had some penetrating appreciation of the beauty of human character—the supreme beauty our world has to offer. I sometimes, no doubt, misplaced my admiration, but on the whole I knew the difference between a pure and beautiful life and a showy but hollow one. I wish I could add music and poetry to the list of beautiful things that helped to build my inner life during these early years. Music was largely left out of the formative years of a Quaker boy. It was a major error, as most Quakers now admit, and I have gone through life missing that important spring of joy and power. I always loved poetry, but I did not "find" the great poetry which would have fed me if I had been exposed to it. We had a few excellent poems in our school Reading Books, nearly all of which I learned by heart, but I was well grown before I had a copy of Longfellow or Whittier or Lowell, and I was still older before Wordsworth and Tennyson and Browning "found" me and made me forever and immeasurably their debtor.

I had no satisfactory theory to explain the presence and the work of God in nature. I find it hard to discover a satisfactory theory even now. But, at any rate, my love of beauty in nature helped very much to strengthen and support my faith in God. I *felt* His presence in my world rather than thought out how He could be there. When I was moved with wonder, awe and mystery, I was always reaching out beyond what I saw and touched, and I had a religious feeling even if I did not have a sound theory to go with it. But my religious faith would have been thin and poor if it had not been for the great Book which from the very beginning formed a chief interest and a major influence in my life. I must tell how I found my way into that priceless possession of the ages.

CHAPTER IV

SEARCHING THE SCRIPTURES

I began to go to Bible School when I was six years old. It was a union school, held on the top floor of a store in a room which had been fitted up as a public hall. I was in a class of little boys, and we were taught by a Friend who knew more about farming than he did about boys, and who sometimes made us laugh with his funny way of talking; but he did us a real service, and I still remember some of the passages in the Psalms which he had us learn "by heart." Learning by heart had not then gone out of fashion, and in our neighborhood the idea was cherished that a well-stored memory might possibly some day prove useful. This was, it will be understood, before the discovery of the method of entertaining children with pretty stories to make the hour interesting. We sat on a hard, straight bench, with our little feet some way from the floor, and said over and over our verses which we had learned during the week. "Whither shall I fly from Thy presence?" was one of the passages; and then our teacher "moralized" to us until the hour was over.

But my real acquaintance with the Bible was made at that best school—a mother's knee. The Bible was our one book at home, and we used it as the scholar uses his library. We literally fed ourselves on it. We began the day with reading it. We read out of it in the evening, and we read it on First-day (Sunday) as part of the business of the day. When I was eight years old I was set to read the Psalms through, with the promise of a new pair of mittens—as strangely colored as Joseph's coat—when the task was done. I faithfully did it, and, what is more, it did me good. I really felt the power of this Hebrew poetry, and I soon got to know the Psalms so that at morning reading I used to call for my favorite ones when mother asked if any one had a "selection."

Two years later—when I was ten—came one of the crises of my life. It was a great misfortune, which turned out to be a blessing, as is usually the case, if one has eyes to see it. It was the injury to my foot, already mentioned, which nearly cost me my leg and seriously threatened my life. Through all the pain and suffering I discovered what a mother's love was. I had been going to the bad all summer. I was finding out the endless resources for fun and mischief which a country village, full of boys and girls, offers, and I had stretched the proverbial apron-string to the breaking point. I had got in the way of doing things which I did not tell at home, and I often hurried away in the morning before I found what the work of the day would be, so that I might have the day on the lake with the boys. Temptations were as thick as bees on the clover, and I let them settle on me without scaring them off. When I came home at night I generally felt hopelessly bad, for I knew I had grieved everybody who loved me; but the next day I did the same thing over again, if I got a chance. This particular misfortune came when I had gone to the lake early First-day morning for a swim, and so did not get back in time to go to meeting with the family.

For nine months I never took a step, and for the first week of my suffering mother sat by me every night, and I felt her love sweep over me. As soon as I was through the racking pain, something had to be done to entertain me—to make the long hours pass, for everybody in our household was occupied with their own tasks. Grandmother, who was eighty-eight years old, had plenty of leisure, and so it was arranged for us to entertain each other. I decided to read the Bible through out loud to her. She could knit mechanically with flying needles, giving no more attention to her fingers than she did to the movement of the hands on the clock. Her hands had learned how to knit until they did it themselves. Lying stretched out by her, I began at the great words, "In the beginning God created," and read on through the wonderful events.

There were many passages which puzzled me and held me up, but between us we generally thought our way through, and we fixed up an explanation which I dare say might not be found in the latest commentary; but perhaps it was as near right as some of the conclusions there given, for it came from the mouth of the little ones whose wisdom Christ commended. The real trial came when I got into a "begat" chapter, and had to read through generations of men who had unpronounceable names. Here grandmother suddenly found that her knitting needed most of her attention, and I had to do the best I could with Chedorlaomer and other persons whose mothers, I thought, showed no taste in the choice of names. But I never skipped anything. I fully believed that one line was just as much inspired as another, and I always had fear of those plagues which were spoken of at the end upon those who put in or left out something.

As soon, however, as we got to the main current, which begins with the call of Abraham, I was carried on by the force of the stream. This was the most interesting thing I had ever read, and I finished

Joseph with tears running down my face. I shall never get over that impression.

Boys nowadays read so many stories, and such highly-spiced ones, full of dramatic situations, that they do not perhaps feel the power of this wonderful picture of the patriarchal life. It is a sad loss to miss it. It more than made up for my lack of other books—and for me these characters were as real and vivid as the people moving in the next room. Every event of Jacob's and Joseph's careers was as clearly pictured as were the things my eyes had seen. Moses' life and deeds in Egypt, and the events of the exodus and wilderness journey were hardly less moving; but I found my passage often impeded in Leviticus, Numbers and Deüteronomy. There was nothing in my world like it. I could not imagine the descriptions. I got dreadfully frightened over eating pork, because the swine did not chew the cud and so had "no standing under the law." Not a person in our neighborhood could explain on what ground we boldly went on eating pork in flat contradiction of the Scriptures! This gave grandmother and me some very hard exegesis, and we never felt that we made a good case.

As a boy I thought Judges a great book. I did not realize then, as I do now, what a crisis this period was in Israel's history, when "every man was doing what was right in his own eyes," but

I was carried along with intense interest over the doings of Deborah, and Gideon, and Jephtha, and Samson. Here my imagination had no such difficulties as it had encountered over Urim and Thummin, and the ark, which I never could quite reconstruct. But David was my hero. He was a man after my own heart. I always had a thrill as Samuel passed all Jesse's sons without finding his king-boy, and finally discovered him off with the sheep, and then came the description of the great battle with Goliath in the "Valley of Elah," which came to be the most familiar scene to me of any recorded in the Old Testament. It was the glory of being God's champion which moved me so, and the fact that a boy from the sheepfold could deliver a nation kindled me. Wherever the narrative grew vivid and great events were done I felt my pulse throb, and, on the other hand, I always suffered over Israel's defeats and sins.

Daniel and Esther were two of my best books, and I knew intimately all the details of their experiences. The prophets, however, were far above me. Elijah and Elisha were all right, but the ones who wrote did not speak to my condition. I knew it must all be wonderful, and I believed that they were speaking for God, but I did not understand what they meant. It was all a puzzle which nobody could solve for me, and it was only much later, when I knew the history which called forth these messages, that I learned to love and appreciate them.

Before I began the New Testament I was well enough to go out, so that my reading stopped, and it was not until much later that I got deeply hold of that message which came from the Master. The Old Testament was the book of my boyhood. My heroes and heroines were there. It gave me my first poetry and my first history, and I got my growing ideas of God from it. The idea of choice, the fact that God chose a people and that He chose individuals for His missions, was rooted in my thought.

It was during this year that a large company of the neighbors met at our house to study the Bible one evening in the week, and I offered to let them question me as long as they wished on any events of the Old Testament, and I did not fail. It was a boyish confidence, which I should not show now, but it will make clear that this Book had been made my own.

But greatly as I loved the Bible and devoutly as I believed in my first years that it was to be taken in literal fashion, I am thankful to say that I very early caught the faith and insight, which George Fox and other Quaker leaders had taught, that God is always revealing Himself, and that truth is not something finished, but something unfolding as life goes forward. In spite of the fact that I lived in a backwoods community into which modern ideas had not penetrated and belonged to an intensely evangelical family, I nevertheless grew up with an attitude of breadth toward Scripture. I searched it, I loved it, I believed it, but I did not think that God stopped speaking to the human race when "the beloved disciple" finished his last book in the New Testament. The very fact that the Spirit of God could impress His thought and will upon holy men of old and had done it made me feel confident that He could continue to do that, and consequently that more light and truth could break through men in our times and in those to come. I cannot be too thankful that that little group of believers who made the Bible my living book and who helped me to find and to love its treasures also had spiritual depth enough to give me the key to a larger freedom that enabled me in later years to keep the Bible still as my book, without at the same time preventing me from making use of all that science and history have revealed or can reveal of God's creative work and of His dealing with men.

I had a small playmate whose father "discovered" perpetual motion. This boy told me that Queen Victoria had offered a prize of one hundred thousand dollars to any person in the world who would succeed in making a "perpetual motion machine" and that his father had had a "revelation" telling him how to do it. This man who had been a shoe maker like Jacob Boehme, and who always spoke or prayed with great fervor in our Quaker meetings, actually got the town in March Town Meeting to exempt from taxation for ten years the mill which he proposed to build and to "run" with his new invention! He stopped shoe making and turned his shop into a laboratory. No one was allowed to enter this realm of mystery and there behind the veil of secrecy this good old man inspired by his dreams and revelations toiled away at his *magnum opus* which was to begin a new epoch of civilization. He expected to have it perfected in time for the Centennial, to be held in Philadelphia, but there was some hitch in the mechanism which caused delay, and the Centennial came and went without the unending device. I was one of the few persons who ever saw it. This playmate of mine took me in one day to see it. I was filled with awe as I stood in the chamber of mystery. The ceiling of the old familiar shop had been cut away and this marvelous machine, which was to win Queen Victoria's prize, had climbed up to the very roof and occupied a good part of the house. It was constructed on a "growing" pattern, and had been altered many times to overcome unforeseen difficulties as they arose. I was told in confidence that it would "work" as soon as the father could get a more perfect set of steel springs that formed a crucial part of the vast structure. The boy proposed to start the monster going so that I could see him perform, and sure enough he did. I was thus the entranced spectator of the "beginning" of perpetual motion. I also saw it end! The great ball which was the initial motor-power set the machine into play, but alas! the steel springs had insufficient elasticity and in about fifteen minutes the steel ball was at rest at a dead center and the infinite stretch of "perpetual" was reduced to a feeble finite. One effect of this experience on me has been to make me suspicious of "revelations" that reveal things contrary to the facts and laws of the universe. I am interested in dreams and visions and openings, but I have learned to trust them only so far as they can be tested and verified. When they launched off into matters which conflict with what we know to be nature's established order, I think of that old perpetual motion machine and grow cautious.

When I was twelve years old I took a step which was in later times to bring important results. I joined our village Library Association. It was naturally enough a tiny library, which, such as it was, owed its existence to the civic spirit and the generosity of such persons as my Uncle Eli, a quiet good man named Ambrose Abbott, and others who did what they could to open intellectual possibilities to the farmer boys and girls of the region. Only members of the Association could take out books to read; so I resolved to become a member. The condition of membership was the payment of a dollar or the presentation of a book worth a dollar or more. I did not have a dollar. In fact, up to that period of my life I had never had a whole dollar at any one time. But we possessed a copy of J. G. Holland's *Life of Abraham Lincoln*. It had cost much more than a dollar of very hard earned money and father told me that I might give it to the library to start my membership. It was a great moment when I was enrolled and could draw out books.

One of the first books I got was *Gulliver's Travels*. It was thrilling for I had never before read a great imaginative creation and I was swept along by the strange doings of the men of Lilliput. But the excitement was soon over, for my dear Aunt Peace, who to my mind never made a mistake before or afterwards, picked it up by accident and quickly decided that I must not read any farther in the book, because she was convinced that it was not "true," and she did not want her boy to read anything that was not "true." I pleaded for my precious story, but all in vain. No argument worked. No urging availed. I was not to spoil my mind with scenes that never happened and never could happen. I was to grow up in the love of truth and not to wander into the realms of fiction and make-believe. I do not blame the dear soul for her decision. It was for the honor of truth, and she could not know then that it is as important to train imagination as it is to learn the multiplication table. I obeyed and took Gulliver back for the wicked little boys of the town to read! And I took out "good" books which told the truth.

One of the most valuable "exercises" of our school was the class in English Grammar. I rose to the distinction of being in the class when I was about thirteen. It met the last "period" of the day, and all who did not belong in it were allowed to go home before this class began to recite. We learned outright all the rules of Brown's Grammar, including the rules of prosody, versification, and scanning. We recited these like parrots and gave an example of each rule. Unfortunately, we did not often succeed in carrying the application of the rules into our daily habits of speech. We knew that the personal pronoun "I" was to be used as subject and that "me" was the objective case, but we went right on saying, "He told John and I to go." We got our heads full of grammatical truth but it did not get carried over into practice until the years taught us. The second half of this grammar period we learned to parse. We always pronounced it "pass," for we never sounded an "r" if it was written! The place where we came in strong on "r" was in words ending in "a," such as "area," or "Anna," which were invariably pronounced with a redundant r—"are*ar*" and "Annar." There was some question in our minds whether the "r" was silent in "dorg"! We usually parsed poetry, and one of my first lessons in parsing consisted of the memorable lines of Milton:

> "Of man's first disobedience and the fruit
> Of that forbidden tree, whose mortal taste
> Brought death into the world and all our woe,
> With loss of Eden, till one greater Man
> Restore us and regain that blissful seat,
> Sing heavenly Muse."

I felt at once the greatness of these lines and surrendered to the spell of that mighty Epic. Then we met for the first with Tennyson's marvelous song:

> "The splendour falls on castle walls
> And snowy summits old in story:
> The long light shakes across the lakes,
> And the wild cataract leaps in glory.
> Blow, bugle, blow, set the wild echoes flying,
> Blow bugle; answer, echoes, dying, dying, dying.

O love, they die in yon rich sky,
They faint on hill or field or river:
Our echoes roll from soul to soul,
And grow forever and forever."

I had almost no idea what this meant. I learned it by heart; I felt the charm of the melody, the march of the meter and the swing of the rhythm, and repeated it again and again with a powerful fascination. Years afterwards, when far away from the old schoolhouse and the parsing class, in a sudden flash, as I was saying the poem over, I *saw* what it meant. Something like that, too, has happened to me with many of my deepest experiences of life and with the discovery of much of the religious truth, by which I have learned to live.

CHAPTER V

THE ENDS OF THE EARTH COME TO OUR HOME

Nobody ever quite realizes how his life is being woven day by day out of myriads of invisible threads. But, in fact, each unnoticed influence and every imperceptible tug up or down which the ordinary daily experiences furnish are silently making the life and shaping its course. The commonplace present we hardly count because we are always looking back on a past or dreaming ahead into a rosy future, which will be full of wonderful and epoch-making events. And yet all the time, in spite of us, the future is being made out of the present, and the stuff of our future is to be what we are now weaving in. We have only to look back to see how true this is. We never really cut loose from our old selves; the threads which the boy wove in are still in the structure when manhood finds him. The tastes we formed, the habits we acquired, the ambitions we fed, the beliefs we grew up in, are still a part of us. All this makes childhood and youth momentously important and critical periods. The river may become a Mississippi and water half a continent, but its whole course will be determined by the tip of the current up at its source.

Among the many influences which went to form and determine my early life—and so in a measure my whole life—I should give a large place to the visits of itinerant Friends who came to us from far and near. It was a novel custom, this constant interchange of gifted ministers. Something like it apparently prevailed in the early Church, as *The Teaching of the Apostles* indicates, and some of the small religious sects at various periods have maintained an extensive intervisitation, but Friends in the first half of the Nineteenth century had developed a form of itinerant ministry which was almost without parallel. It was an admirable method, especially for our rural neighborhoods. We were isolated, and without this contact with the great world we should have had a narrow ingrowing life, but through this splendid spiritual cross-fertilization, we had a chance to increase and improve the quality of our life and thought. The ends of the earth came to our humble door. We got into living contact with Quaker faith and thought in every land where "our religious Society," as we called it, had members. These visitors brought us fresh messages, but, what was not less important, they were themselves unique personalities and were full of incidents and traveler's lore, and thus they formed an excellent substitute for the books which we lacked. They spoke with a prestige and influence which home people seldom have, and they brought a contribution into my life which I can hardly overestimate.

Our little local group also had its outgoing stream of itinerant ministry and I was almost as much interested in hearing the story of experiences related by our returning members as I was in listening to the strangers who came among us from afar. My great-uncle drove in his carriage at least twice from Maine to Ohio and Indiana on religious visits, visiting families and attending meetings as he went and living much of the time on his journey in his own carriage. My Aunt Peace made many journeys to remote regions in America and brought back vast stores of information and wisdom. Uncle Eli and Aunt Sybil, who in my youth were among the foremost living Quakers in gift and power of ministry, went back and forth like spiritual shuttles, now weaving their strands of truth into our lives and now again weaving in some far away spot of the earth. It was a very common and ordinary matter for New England Friends to drive to "the Provinces," especially to Nova Scotia, on religious visits, and, as soon as the railroads made travel easy and rapid, there was an almost unbroken stream of this circulating ministry. Those who came were frequently strangely unlike our native, home-born folks, with different habits and manners and with unusual accents of speech. Some possessed marked culture and refinement, and brought with them a luminous trail of spiritual light, while some were hardly able to construct a sentence which did not violate the ordinary rules of grammar. Some who came had the arresting accent of the Erin-born, another betrayed his Norse origin, a third talked in the speech of the mid-western prairies. One stammered and another had no palate to his mouth but both had heavenly grace and unmistakable power.

One man I remember even now as vividly as though I still saw him standing up to speak in his pepper-gray suit of clothes. He spoke with marked English accent, with well-chosen words, notable insight, sure vision, and convincing power. I did not take my eyes from his face or miss a word. He was engaged on a tour of all the Quaker meetings in America, even the most remote ones, and wherever he went he left memorable results behind him. His visit had been foretold by a prophetic woman from America, who, speaking in London yearly meeting, before he had announced his call to service, declared that someone was present there in the meeting whom the Lord was calling to an extensive service abroad. Then in a solemn voice she added, "it is laid upon me to urge him to make haste for his time is short." In my later life an English Friend told me that he was sitting in this meeting, when this happened, on the same bench on which the man himself was sitting to whom the woman referred. The bench trembled so violently that all who were sitting on it knew that it contained the one to whom the call had come. Hardly was the extensive tour of service finished when the earthly life of this gifted man came to an end and that circumstance gave vivid emphasis to those never forgotten words, "the time is short."

These gospel travelers all came from a world as unknown to me as was the jungle of Africa, and they were beings of a high order and rare species, to be gazed upon with wonder and listened to with awe. It is not easy to explain why a person who comes from a place a thousand miles away should impress one so much more than an equally good person whom one meets every day, but the fact remains. Familiarity does play havoc with us all. The prophet always dwells somewhere else than where we have settled. He is always in another town, in another state—never one of the well-known figures of our own neighborhood. These men and women who seemed so wonderful to me were not lights of the first magnitude, but when they came into our horizon like a new star, with no known history to judge them by, I always believed them to be remarkable persons, and very often they were such.

Then, too, I felt a certain awe because they always came with "a concern," which means that they had left their homes and had undertaken the long journey because they had received an unmistakable and irresistible call to go out and preach what was given them. This was no ordinary visit. Here was a man under our roof who had come because God sent him. I supposed that he had something inside which had told him to go, and where to go, and that this "something inside" told him exactly what to say when he spoke to us. In my childish thought I put these "beloved brothers with minutes" in a very high class, with an inspiration only a little below that which the writers of the Bible possessed. That I took this view was partly due to the fact that so many of them "spoke to the state and condition" of some one either in our family or in the neighborhood. These visiting ministers had a way of seeing through your life and of prophesying your future, which made one solemn when they spoke.

While a company of neighbors were gathered in our sitting-room where a Friend of this authoritative sort had been sitting in silence, he quietly rose and asked a man in the room to stand up. He then asked a woman who was present to stand by the side of the man. With deep reverence and solemnity, he said: "I think that will do, and I believe it has the divine approval." Not long after, this couple, thus encouraged, were joined in marriage, and entered upon a union which was much blessed. Nobody thought of this in a light way. It was taken as an undoubted expression of the will of God.

Not far from us a visiting Friend of great weight and power was holding a meeting by appointment. A large company came to hear him because he had a remarkable gift. One man in the community who had the reputation of being a skeptic had not gone. This man got on horseback and started for the village by a road which passed the one that led into the meeting-house. As he rode along he felt irresistibly impressed that he ought to go to meeting, but he would not give in. As he came near the junction of the roads he threw the reins on the horse's neck, and resolved to go whichever way the horse took him. Contrary to his well-formed habit, the horse turned in at the meeting-house, and the man went into the meeting.

The house was full, and the minister was in the midst of a powerful sermon. The man dropped into a seat by the door, as much unnoticed as possible. Suddenly the minister stopped, fixed his eye, and said, "So thou decided to leave it to thy horse. It would have been well to have left it to the horse years ago." Then he preached a direct and searching sermon, which reached this man's life and changed the whole current of his thought.

These were no rare and isolated incidents. Such things were frequent. One Friend in particular, who used to come from a distant yearly meeting, was strikingly gifted to see into the hidden secrets of the heart, and I had an unquestioning belief in her power to read a life. Another Friend—this time from England—had astonished everybody at monthly meeting by preaching a sermon which unfolded the condition of a prominent member of the meeting so plainly that it seemed as though God had sent a direct message.

All these things worked upon me and impressed me; and then, still further, these far-traveled visitors would sit by our hearth and tell of their remarkable experiences in other places—how the Lord had sent them out with nothing and had provided for them, or how they had been led into strange and unexpected service, or how they had felt out the condition of some family or meeting which they had visited—until I learned to believe that ministers, at least those that came from a distance, were, if not little lower than angels, then surely considerably higher than ordinary mortals. I have never since seen one of these persons who were the prophets of my childhood without adding something to him for memory's sake, and, as I listened, his words meant more to me than they otherwise would, because I colored them with my childish belief that he must be greater and more gifted than other persons—for had not God sent him to us?

Whenever such visitors as I have been describing came we had an "opportunity," or a "tunity," as we children named it, when we were too small to pronounce both ends of a long word. The choice of this word indicates a happy insight and shrewd wisdom on the part of those who used the word, for an "opportunity," put in plain, cold language, was nothing more or less than a religious meeting held in the home by the ministering Friend, who was "visiting families." It never was quite settled in my mind whether it was an "opportunity" for the visitor or for the family, but it always made a sharp and immediate break with whatever we were doing at the time. If we were playing when the word came, the game was left half finished; if we were working, the task was interrupted, and we all gathered in the little sitting-room with the visitor, who had come from far with a "concern" for us.

Not infrequently I heard my own name spoken as the minister raised his voice in prayer, and God was asked by this special servant of His to help me. I knew that such a prayer would count, and I always felt more confidence in myself after this kind of an "opportunity" was over.

But I half feared, too, that some of these penetrating souls would see how very bad I was, and how impossible it was for me to keep good very long. One Friend came who went to sleep on our sitting-room sofa, and in her sleep suddenly began to preach. We were all called in and for more than half an hour she poured forth a remarkable gospel message, which filled me with awe, and when she woke up she had no knowledge that she had said anything. This greatly increased my faith in the Bible stories which told how God showed things in dreams.

Once a dear, saintly man, who was as graceful and courtly as though he had been a knight of Arthur's Round Table, and whose kindly face has been a benediction to thousands, came to visit us. He brought with him a young man who had run away from the Southern army because he could not fight, and who afterwards became a Friend. They were both most unusual men, and I had hardly stirred while I was listening to their words, which fascinated me and moved me. The saintly man walked over to me and put his hands on my head, and slowly announced his prophecy about me. I was then ten years old. What he said would ordinarily have made little impression. But I fully believed that he knew what he was saying, and the words remained with me as an inspiration long after the man himself had forgotten that he spoke them. They have since been fulfilled in every respect.

I am not now concerned with the influence of these itinerant ministers in the public meeting which they attended. That must wait for a later chapter. I am speaking only of the personal influence in the homes that they visited. They told us of life and work in far-off lands. They interested us with their narratives, and in our narrow life they performed somewhat the service of the wandering minstrel in the days of the old castles. They gave us new experiences, a touch of wider life and farther-reaching associations, and for me, at least, they made the connection with God more real. I got from them a clearer sense of what I might be, and it was largely because I believed that men and women had been sent from remote lands to visit us that I was so sure that we were a "chosen people."

CHAPTER VI

MINISTRY AND SILENCE

Never again in this world will any one see such a meeting as the one to which I went twice in the week, after I was old enough to sit upright in a seat. Such a meeting will not be seen again simply because the kind is passing away, and because the characters who composed it were absolutely original and unique and not to be matched anywhere. The meeting-house was a plain wooden building, with unpainted seats, and divided into two equal halves by wooden "shutters," which could be raised or lowered to make two rooms or one of the house as occasion required. Along the front ran two elevated seats, one above the other—called the "high seats" —where the ministers and elders sat, facing the body of the house. We lived three miles from the meeting-house, over a rocky, hilly road running all the way through woods. The question, however, was never raised whether we should or should not go to meeting, any more than it was whether we should or should not have dinner. Even the horse knew that he was foreordained to these bi-weekly trips, and to his long, quiet wait in the meeting-house "shed." The house was well filled—men on one side and women on the other. All the women past middle life wore the long, stiff, flaring bonnet, covered with grey silk, with a cape behind, which was the mark of good standing in our Quaker community. The elder ones wore underneath a dainty white muslin cap. The men of our meeting had no set dress, though one or two ancient Friends had broad beaver hats and collarless coats, which brought down to our time the garb of sanctity which prevailed a generation before.

There were two rows of "high-seat" Friends on each side, and though none of them had been to "Oxford or Cambridge," nor, I may add, to any institution more advanced than a common country school, there were some of God's anointed minsters in that little group. The one who "sat at the head" on the men's side and the one who occupied the similar place on the women's side had been to the Holy Land, and when I began to go to meeting, had recently returned from that land, all fresh with the impressions which their travels had made upon them, and full of living, vivid pictures of the scenes where the great events in the world's spiritual history had come to pass. They both had a marvelous power of interesting listeners, and they fixed attention both by message and manner. These were Eli and Sybil Jones, my revered uncle and aunt. Uncle Eli was my father's oldest brother. He was a man of very superior intellectual power and of rare spiritual qualities. He had extremely scant school education, but he was a diligent reader and student all his life, and he revealed almost no indication of his lack of early training. He was an intimate friend of John Greenleaf Whittier and John Bright and of many other distinguished persons of his time, but with all his travels and his contacts with important men in this and other lands, he remained a simple country farmer with a meager income, and he seemed to be content to pour his life and spirit into the people of our rural community. His leadership, his inspiration, and his friendship were beacon influences in my early years.

His wife, Sybil, possessed a touch of genius. Always delicate in health, severely limited in physical strength, she had a spirit of vast scope and range. She constantly transcended herself and spoke with a wisdom and power not her own. She seemed to be *made* for a great career of service and she rose to the full height of her possibilities—and a little more. Uncle Eli spoke more often from the Old Testament, and, in his original, eloquent style, made some one of the characters live and act his part before our eyes. His wife, with a voice of mingled softness and power, and a grace that a queen might have envied, generally made the story of redeeming love her theme, and she preferred to follow the steps of the "blessed feet" from the early days in Nazareth until they were pierced on Calvary. She often saw tears glisten in the corner of eyes as she spoke. I was a boy, and I loved the story of David and his daring deeds, or the dramatic course of Joseph in Egypt, better. I understood it all, and I knew that I would have done the same thing—if I had dared! I used to feel my whole self go out in interest as I followed these descriptions.

They both made sin awfully real, and they left no shadow of doubt of its ultimate effect, but the striking note of their preaching was the beauty and joy and peace which the true life gives. They made religion attractive. They told the story of the cross so that I felt its power. In every sermon there would break out some great word about the meaning and possibility of life, until, boy as I was, I wanted to be something and do something to show that I appreciated such love.

There was also in this "high-seat" group a woman who wore the white flower of a holy life. She had passed through deep trials, and had tasted bitter cups, but she had won her way into the secrets of the Lord. She lacked some qualities which a public speaker needs, but her inward grace and daily converse with her Lord more than made up for the lack. Her ministry was convincing beyond all argument, and her rising or kneeling always left a fragrance which lasted after meeting broke. This was my Aunt Peace. She was much greater as a *person* than she was as a preacher, though at her best, as I have said, she spoke effectively. But take her life day by day, in the simple round of duties and contacts, I have never seen any one of richer or purer or nobler personal quality. She had a refinement which ran far ahead of her environment and breeding. She had moral intuition which was almost uncanny, and with it a grace and gentleness that made her a sweet and persuasive guide. Some man missed a treasure when he let her live her life in single blessedness, but he rendered me a great favor in leaving this pure flower to bloom in our home and to shed its fragrance on our lives.

On the other side of the "gallery seats" was one who spoke with an Irish accent, who had come among us from across the seas and had married the daughter of my Uncle Eli and Aunt Sybil. He too had come up through hard and trying experiences, but the furnace of trial had added a new quality to the temper of his character and he bore in his face and spirit the marks of his victory. He had rare powers of speech, was full of striking incidents, apt with illustrations, and always ready with a poetic passage which fitted his theme. To him I listened as a child listens to a loved story. This gifted man had a son just my own age, who soon became as dear to me as a brother. Our lives were later to be bound together in the closest way during our years of boarding school and college life, and forever after. The fact that this cousin of mine was to be at meeting, as he always was, added a new attraction and drawing force, and in the course of time we sat together in meeting and started that wonderful fellowship which meant so much to the lives of us both.

Very often in these meetings, which held usually for nearly two hours, there were long periods of silence, for we never had singing to fill the gaps. I do not think anybody ever told me what the silence was for. It does not seem necessary to explain Quaker silence to children. They *feel* what it means. They do not know how to use very long periods of hush, but there is something in short, living, throbbing times of silence which *finds* the child's submerged life and stirs it to nobler living and holier aspiration. I doubt if there is any method of worship which works with a subtler power or which brings into operation in the interior life a more effective moral and spiritual culture. Sometimes a real spiritual wave would sweep over the meeting in these silent hushes, which made me feel very solemn and which carried me—careless boy though I was—down into something which was deeper than my own thoughts, and gave me a momentary sense of that Spirit who has been the life and light of men in all ages and in all lands. Nobody in this group had ever heard the word "mystical," and no one would have known what it meant if it had been applied to this form of worship, but in the best sense of the word this was a mystical religion, and all unconsciously I was being prepared to appreciate and at a later time to interpret the experience and the life of the mystics.

But I have been speaking of our meeting as though it were somewhat ideal—a place where only uplifting and edifying words were heard, and where we were all baptized into the unity of the one Spirit. Alas, the millennium was still a good way off, and the checkerboard condition of life, which we all know so well—with squares of black as well as squares of white—prevailed here also. I doubt if any small company of individuals ever had a larger share of "peculiar" persons. The New Englander who has been unspoiled by city influences is almost always "original"—different from everybody else. He is very apt to adopt some pet idea, and rock and feed it until it possesses him. He will have his own quaint way of telling it, but let him start where he may, he is sure to come round to it and give it voice. Once let such a person settle down into an idea and a peculiar way of expressing it, one might almost as well try to change the path of the zodiac as to get him out of his rut. Our meeting was richly supplied with characters who travelled round and round their single truth, their mighty discovery, until we knew every turn and twist in their mental windings. No sermon could possibly be preached which did not start off one or more of these tethered souls around the beaten path of his favorite idea. They each felt that the other's idea was wrong, or empty, and that the meeting was not edified by it, and each one of them felt that the coming together was not entirely profiable unless he had unburdened his spirit and rolled his great truth on the meeting. They all had funny ways of speaking and making gestures—curious expressions appeared from time to time, and the frequent repetition of them only made them sound more odd.

One of these characters wore a strange and remarkable garb, which he believed was required of him, and this added to the quaintness of his speaking, which of itself was queer almost beyond belief. Three sisters in our congregation wore bloomers, a custom which they felt was required of them by their conscience and the laws of health. I used to watch to see them come in and stride up the aisle, wondering whether they would sit with the men or the women. One odd man always sat with a large Bible under him, as though to protect himself from invisible forces from below, and he always kept his mouth moving as though he was biting something. One Friend stood up while prayer was being offered, and one kneeled, the rest of us reverently bowed our heads. One strange looking person came only seldom, but when he did come he spoke of the goodness of the Lord to him, saying with much emotion, "I have a large circle of friends. It takes me a year to visit them all"! Everybody knew then that the visitor had come on his annual rounds and that all would have their turn. Another visitor from a nearby meeting could always be counted on to say, "Now I am reminded of the dying words of the pious Addison," and he was apt to warn us of our worldliness by powerfully intoning the ominous words, "Jeshurun waxéd fat and kickéd."

All this was a hard test on a boy. Imitation is one of the earliest instincts. From the first smile of the baby the imitative instinct works. It is almost impossible not to imitate odd and curious ways, and we children used to play meeting, and act over and over the characteristic things which we heard, until it got ever more difficult to sit through them with sober faces. The most wonderful thing, however, was the patience and the grace of the weighty members of the meeting in dealing with these situations. They held rigidly to the freedom of speech. The difference between the great gospel message which came from one of the saints of the meeting and the queer deliverance which often proceeded from the odd prophets of a single idea was remarkable. But the meeting steadfastly gave the latter his opportunity. It was plainly a trial, but the jarring notes only made it all the more necessary for the spiritual members to do their part to make the tone of the meeting high. Their faith in the power of truth, their saintly patience and gentleness under difficulties, had their effect upon us all, and we got so that we could pass from the soul-stirring sermon on "Who is this that cometh from Edom, with dyed garments from Bozrah?" to the weird, shrill words, "I wonder what difference it makes what *we* think. The question ain't whether or no, or not, *we* think so; no, not by no means?" and feel almost no shock. Gradually we learned to get the good and to pass the other by.

CHAPTER VII

THE SENSE OF THE MEETING

"If Friends' minds are easy, I apprehend it may now be a suitable time to lower the shutters and proceed to the business of the meeting." As the venerable elder at the head of the meeting spoke these words, slowly and solemnly, he raised his broad-brim and put it on his head with considerable dignity, and we children knew that the "first meeting" was over. In these modern days a dinner is served "between the meetings," but in my boyhood days no such thing ever happened. Not even the hungry boy got a bite until the affairs of the church were properly settled. Creak, creak, creak—we heard the middle "shutters" coming down from above to divide the men from the women. I could never imagine how it was done! No human instrument was ever anywhere visible. The ancient elder spoke, and lo, the wonder worked! Later, when the investigating age was upon me, I crawled up a ladder into the loft and solved the mystery; but in the early period it seemed as though the same spirit which "moved" the solemn man to put on his hat was also in the descending shutters, which no visible hand touched.

It was Uncle Stephen who sat "at the head of the meeting" and who "apprehended." He was one of the most dignified and kindly solemn persons I have ever seen. He would have graced the Vatican and might have presided without a flaw at a papal conclave. He was nearly six feet and four inches tall, straight as Trafalgar monument and dressed with the last touch of Quaker precision. Every garment he wore reminded one of Barclay's Apology and William Penn's Holy Experiment. I never knew how he could be a farmer and milk cows, and still look as though he had spent the entire week in a bandbox. Every word he spoke was weighed and balanced before he uttered it. Exaggeration would have shocked him as much as an oath. He always understated: "I think, or at least I think that I think"! But when, finally, after everybody had spoken and some had gone off at half-cock, he slowly rose, until from the high seat his head nearly reached the ceiling, and said his few chosen words which weighed a ton—there was nothing more for anybody to say!

I used always to sit on the "men's side," but I sat close up by the partition, and ever and anon I caught the notes of a woman's voice breaking in upon our "business" with a strong outpouring of prayer or the earnest word of counsel, for the women had less "business" than the men, and hence "religious exercises" filtered all through their "second meeting." It was somewhat so on the men's side, though to a less extent. But even here it was impossible to draw any line between "business" and "religious exercises." A solemn religious tinge colored everything, even the driest items of business, and I believe the spiritual tide often rose higher in the "second meeting" than in the first—particularly if there was a visiting minister present.

By the world's method, all our business could have been transacted in twenty minutes. We often spent two hours at it, because every affair had to be soaked in a spiritual atmosphere until the dew of religion settled on it! Above in the "high seats," sat two men at a table fastened by hinges to the minister's rail. This table was swung up and held by a perpendicular stick beneath. On it lay the old record-book, a copy of the "discipline," and papers of all sorts. The "clerk," the main man of the two at the desk, was another of those marvelous beings who seemed to me to know everything by means of something unseen working inside him! How could he tell what "Friends" wanted done? —and yet he always knew. No votes were cast. Everybody said something in his own peculiar way. A moment of silence would come, and the clerk would rise and say, "It appears that it is the sense of the meeting" to do thus and so. Spontaneously from all parts of the house would come from variously-pitched voices—"I unite with that," "So do I," "That is my mind," "I should be easy to have it so." And so we passed to the next subject.

Occasionally there would be a Friend who had "a stop in his mind," or who "didn't feel easy" to have things go as the rest believed they should go. If he were a "weighty Friend," whose judgment had been proved through a long past, his "stop" would effectually settle the matter; but if he were a persistent and somewhat cantankerous objector, the clerk would quietly announce that the "weight of the meeting" seemed decidedly favorable to action.

The longest stretch of business was always over the "queries." These were original inventions of the Quaker, and they have no parallel in any other religious body. Like many other things, the "queries," with their carefully rendered answers, have undergone a change. They take a less important place now, and the boy of to-day may not tell of them when he gives his impressions to the next generation. But in my day they were still alive and the meeting took them seriously enough.

"Are all meetings regularly held?" "Are Friends careful to observe the hour?" "Do Friends keep from all unbecoming behavior therein?" "Are love and unity maintained?" "Are tale-bearing and detraction guarded against?" "Do Friends pay their bills, settle their accounts and live within the bounds of their circumstances?" "Do they read the Holy Scriptures in their families, and bring up their children in the nurture and admonition of the Lord?" "If differences arise, are measures taken to end them speedily?" "Is the discipline administered timely and impartially?"

Each separate meeting sent its special set of answers for this public confessional. "Love and unity are not so well maintained as we could wish." "Some Friends do not observe the hour." "Mostly kept from unbecoming behavior, though a few cases of sleeping in meeting have been observed." "Friends generally bring up their children in the nurture and admonition of the Lord." I had no idea what that meant, though I assumed it meant "to be good."

After the answers were read, we listened to grave preachments on these various lines which "were queried after," as the phrase used to run. What got said on these occasions was not very juicy food for a boy, though the standard of life which was set up in these times of examination did, after all, have a silent influence which left a good deposit behind.

There were two transactions which were always exciting, and I used each time to live in hope that they would come off. One was "the declaration of intentions of marriage." When such an event occurred the man and woman came in and sat down together, facing the meeting in the completest possible hush. It was an ordeal which made the couple hesitate to rush into marriage until they felt pretty sure that the match was made in heaven. Solemnly they rose, and informed us that they purposed taking each other in marriage, and the parents announced their consent. The meeting "united" and permission was given "to proceed." The marriage itself came off at an even more solemn meeting, when the man and woman took each other "until death should separate." I remember one of these occasions, when the frightened groom took the bride "to be his husband," which made the meeting less solemn than usual.

The other interesting event was the liberation of ministers for religious service "in other parts." If the minister were a woman Friend, as often happened in our meeting, she came in from the other side with "a companion." They walked up the aisle and sat down with bowed heads. Slowly the bonnet strings were untied, the bonnet handed to the companion, and the ministering woman rose to say that for a long time the Lord had been calling her to a service in a distant yearly meeting; that she had put it off, not feeling that she could undertake so important a work, but that her mind could not get any peace; and now she had come to ask Friends to release her for this service. One after another the Friends would "concur in this concern," and the blessing of the Lord would be invoked upon the messenger who was going forth.

Some of these occasions were of a heavenly sort, and the voices of strong men choked in tears as a beloved brother or sister was equipped and set free. From this little meeting heralds went out to almost every part of the world, and the act of liberation was something never to be forgotten, and only to be surpassed by the deep rejoicing which stirred the same company when the journey was over and "the minutes were returned."

It is all very well now to sit down at a comfortable desk and write of what happened in those long business meetings. But the kind reader will please remember that the uncushioned seats were hard in those days, and that a boy's stomach will not be fed with "considerations on the state of the church"! Long before the "concluding minute" was read a rebellion was well under way within. The vivid picture of that steaming dinner which was (to the boy) the real event of those days, blotted out the importance of preserving love and unity, or any of the other desirable things which concerned the elders. At length the happy moment came—"We now separate, proposing to meet again at the usual time and place, if the Lord permit."

With this began the invasion of the homes in the neighborhood. Every dining-room had its long table, and an elastic supply to fit the rather reckless invitations which all members of the family gave with little or no consultation. Here was one place where a boy counted as much as a man! In the meeting he had no part to play, he was not considered, but the havoc he wrought on the dinner made him a person of some importance! If he got crowded out to the second table the delay only made him a more dangerous element to reckon with!

No boy who has had the fortune of being taken to monthly or quarterly meeting in the good old days of positive religion and genuine hospitality will forget what it meant, so long as he remembers anything.

CHAPTER VIII

THE TREE OF KNOWLEDGE

God was just as real a being to me all through my early boyhood as was any one of the persons in our nearest neighbor's house. At home He was talked with every morning, and spoken of all day in a variety of ways. If any sort of crisis was near us His help was asked, in as simple and confident a way as we asked a neighbor's help when we needed it. Once when a great danger was all day threatening to fall upon our family, we quietly met in the living-room and sat down together, and asked God to deliver us from our trouble. Then mother took the Bible, and allowed it to open of itself to a chapter which was meant for us. It opened to the ninety-first Psalm, and I can still remember the thrill which went over me and the confidence which rose up in me as she read, "There shall no evil befall thee, neither shall any plague come nigh thy dwelling." No one of us for a moment doubted these words. They came as though they had been spoken directly to us from the sky, and they proved true.

A hundred things which occurred convinced me that God was a real person, who took care of us, who knew all about us, and who was all the time near by. Again and again I was told to do some particular thing because "God wanted me to do it," or not to do something because "God would not like to have me do it." "How does thee think God will feel?" were the words which met me when I had done wrong.

Now this overwhelming conviction that I was more closely and immediately under God's care and observation than I was under the eye of the teacher in the little schoolroom where almost no act escaped notice, would have been very comforting if I had always been good. I really did enjoy thinking, when I had in a rare moment done a good thing, that God was seeing it and liking me for it. But, alas, the balance was always on the wrong side! I meant to be good. I knew I ought to be. Almost from babyhood I had been told that God wanted to use me in His service, but spite of everything I was forever finding myself in the wrong path.

The happy period of innocence—the brief lease of the garden of Eden which, all unconsciously, every child has—was for me soon over. The first mouthful of the apple from the tree of knowledge of good and evil is back of the period of memory, but as far back as I can go I find my Eden very badly lost. No day in that little life of mine was without its pangs, and many of them gave me a real terror. My whole upbringing had given me a quick, sensitive and tender heart, a most exalted idea of duty, a keen vision of the good life, and, as I have said, a certainty that God was entering all my acts and doings in His great books. In my good moments no boy ever was better, and the casual visitor put me down as a model boy—perhaps as almost too good to grow up.

But in reality I was a typical sinner. I did precisely the things I knew I ought not to. I can plainly remember walking straight ahead in a sinful course with every string of my conscience tugging at my heart to pull me back. As soon as I got with "the other boys" I let the din of their suggestions of attractive things drown out the low whispers of the tender heart, and we did the things which boys usually do. It went all right while the excitement lasted, and, at a pinch, I easily became the leader in some desperate undertaking, but on the way home alone I became uncomfortable and low-spirited. It was not so much that I disliked the sure questioning which would come, and that I should find difficulty in showing that my day had been spent in an edifying way, but it was rather a deep, dull feeling that I had gone back on my true self, and that I had broken faith with the One Person who knew me altogether.

Socrates taught that "knowledge is virtue," by which he meant that an individual always follows his insight and does as well as he knows. Evil is always due to ignorance. No person ever goes against his better judgment. Socrates may have been one of those rare beings who are so well organized and controlled that they *do* right as soon as they know what *is* right. But as a boy I refuted Socrates' theory a hundred times. What Socrates forgot was that a person is never quite completely rationalized. There are other springs of action in us besides those which our reason furnishes. Instincts and emotions are forces too, and they carry us where rational angels would fear to tread! I am glad now that I was not one of those rational angels. I am glad that I was human and had to learn my way by experience, by trial and error, by the collision of lower and higher forces, until I got "organized" and formed within a set of governing habits which were dependable. The process is a slow one and the period is a perilous time.

Some day, I predict, we shall have a type of education which makes fathers and mothers and teachers experts in this difficult business. If we studied these problems of moral formation in the same patient, painstaking way in which men have studied the nature of atoms and the structure and habits of microbes, we should be able to throw much light on this stupendous business of "organization and control," but at present it is a haphazard affair, guided by very little expert wisdom. In any case, there was no psychological lore at my disposal. I had a great battle on, but I had small stock of fighting tactics to draw upon. I was not depraved, but I was loaded with energy, vivacity and what we now call "urges." I was not vicious, but I was crude and unformed. I never used a "swear word" in my life, though most of the boys with whom I played used very vigorous phrases as a regular part of their vocabulary. I did join, however, with quite natural ease, in the village gossip and vulgarity. I am glad to feel that it did not taint my soul but was only surface talk and a form of cheap humor. But the early adolescent years were full of strain and turmoil.

One of my most frequent companions was many years older than I was. He had had a wild youth, had been in various cities, had served a term in prison, and knew the ways of the world. We sailed the lake together, often staying becalmed out late at night. He was full of anecdotes, lively, jovial, humorous, fascinating. I was flattered by his companionship and formed a real affection for him. He might have led me astray, and most of the critics of the neighborhood were sure that he would be my ruin, but he did me no harm. On the contrary, I believe it was an advantage to me to have had that experience at a time when home influences were pulling me strongly in the right direction. I am thankful now for the sensitive soul which made my deviations and slips seem more sinful then than they really were, but at the time I was forever engaged in a battle of moral issues. Sometimes I lost and sometimes I won. Sometimes the issue was a trivial one and sometimes it was momentous.

My little brother Herbert and I one day were helping father push the mowing machine. Herbert was only four, and in his desire to help he got his finger in the cogs of the wheel. The finger was crushed and the end cut off. I was sent for the doctor, while father carried the poor child to the house. What I remember most vividly is the constant cry that first night after the accident: "Oh, I wish I hadn't done it; I wish I hadn't done it"! Many times I felt those same words on my own lips after I had done "fool things," or mean things, or things which seemed to me "bad." "I wish I hadn't done it"! Almost every time I read the Bible I opened to some passage which just hit my case. I felt sure the passage was meant for me, and in my fear I would resolve to be good all the rest of my days. Aunt Peace understood me like a book. Her wise talks with me revealed to me my better self and fired me with high resolves to "be the thing I mean." But any slight, easy temptation would break every fence I had so painfully builded, and I would find myself off again in the enemy's pasture.

My outside life was just like that of any healthy, growing boy. I played boy's games, learned to swim and dive, sail and fish, hunt and skate, and in the times between I went to school and worked on the farm. It looked from the outside as though this made up the whole of my life. But looked at from within, my life was mostly an invisible battle. More real than the snow fort which we stormed amid a flight of snowballs until we dislodged the possessors of it, was this unseen stronghold of an enemy, who was dislodged only to come back into his fort stronger than ever, so that my assaults seemed fruitless and vain.

When he was a boy on the frontier, going through a similar struggle, Abraham Lincoln wrote on his home-made Arithmetic these verses:

"Abraham Lincoln,
His book and pen:
He will be good,
But God knows when."

I know precisely how he felt. There was something unmistakably pushing him toward goodness, but there was always an undertow that drew mightily in the opposite direction. It is the cry of the hero in Tennyson's "Maud":

> "Ah for a man to arise in me,
> That the man I am might cease to be."

All the time those looking on saw only a careless boy, drifting into the ways of the reckless, thoughtless crowd of village boys who seemed to have no conscience, no fear of God or man. How little one knows what goes on deep within the heart or how sensitive the soul may be when the acts indicate only a hardened nature! At no period of life have I more earnestly longed to be good than in the dark days of growing self-will when I seemed the worst. What a problem, to deal with a boy so as to reach this deeper, truer self which seems lost, and help him to find himself and something better than himself!

The turning point, though by no means the attainment, came for me in a very simple incident—of blessed memory. I had gone a step farther than usual, and had done something which grieved everybody at home, and I expected a severe punishment, which was administered with extreme infrequency in our home. To my surprise my mother took me by the hand and led me to my room; then she solemnly kneeled down by me, and offered a prayer which reached the very inmost soul of me, and reached also the real Helper. No holy of holies would ever have seemed to the pious Jew more awful with the presence of God than that chamber seemed to me. It was one thing to hear prayer in the meeting-house, or in the assembled family, but quite another thing to hear my own case laid before God in words which made me see just what I was, and no less clearly what I ought to be, and what with His help I might be. I learned that day what a mother was for! And though I was still far from won, I was at least where I could more distinctly feel the thread between my soul and the Father, quiver and draw me.

CHAPTER IX

THE WATERSHED

I hesitate to speak of such sacred things as inward experiences, but it is manifestly impossible to touch the heart of one's religion, even in boyhood, without a few words of personal confession. They shall be as simple, direct and honest as I can make them. From the nature of the case the events of one's inward life are too private and personal to be really "described"; the most that one can do is to hint at what has gone on within, and to give some "signs" which others may interpret as best they can from their own experience.

I have already told how, little by little, I found myself living a divided life. I was utterly dissatisfied with myself, and yet I did not know what had happened. Somehow I had passed a boundary. I was no longer a careless, happy-go-lucky boy, satisfied if only I had enough to eat and could play as many hours as I wanted to. There was a flaming sword at every path which led back to the old Eden of peaceful, innocent, happy childhood. Nobody understood me any more, but the worst of it was that I did not in the least understand myself. I gave up all hope of growing good. It was no use trying. I simply could not succeed. The harder I tried the more I knew I was failing. My conscience was as sensitive as a compass needle; it felt every deviation and recorded every sin, but there was no great ground swell within which kept me moving toward righteousness. I was in very truth a double personality, for I hated sin. I loved goodness. I knew how awful it was to waste my life, and yet I went to bed night after night with the heavy feeling upon me that I was farther than ever from my goodness, and frightened at my day's list of failures.

I never talked with any one about my troubles, and I do not believe those nearest me realized that I was having a crisis, for there was no outward sign of it. This whole situation, now so hard to describe clearly, would hardly be worth telling about, and would certainly not here come to light, if it were not for the fact that it is an experience which is well-nigh universal, and one which needs more attention than it usually gets.

There is in one's early life a whole series of budding periods when some new hunger or desire suddenly sprouts out into a strange activity. Some new capacity dawns and demands a career for itself. The impulse to suck is of course the earliest. The desire to kick the little legs and to crow almost overmasters a healthy baby. Without any forewarning, the budding moment comes for creeping, and this most primitive mode of travel has its triumphant course. It would apparently last for life did not a new impulse bud which introduces a better kind of locomotion. There is now an indescribable stirring in the legs, which is the sign that the hour has come to teach walking. More miraculous still is the hatching out of the first word which gives voice to the little soul within. This is a veritable crisis, and it is little use to try to teach speaking until this budding moment has come, when the tiny spirit asserts his right to be heard!

But now there comes much later a still more critical budding period. The small individual self begins to discover his incompleteness, and to yearn, however vaguely, for that Life in which he can find fulfillment. His real hunger for God has dawned, and he makes at the same time the painful discovery of his own littleness. He no more knows just what it is he wants than he did when he had the blind desire to suck. He suffers without knowing what his trouble is. The more passionate his longing for the infinite Companionship the more keen is the conviction of weakness and sin which settles upon him, until he believes he is lost; just as that nameless sadness on the face of a teething child gives the impression that he believes the universe is against him.

Now, the reason that this particular budding crisis, when the spiritual life is dawning, is so much more serious than the previous ones, is that we know so little how to deal with it, and if it is not dealt with in the right way the whole life will be dwarfed or twisted out of its proper course. We can show the child how to walk, but we bungle when we come to the problem of helping a soul make his adjustment with the infinite. Then, too, what succeeds gloriously with one such person proves just the wrong method of approach with another.

While I was in this crisis—with an old self not dead and a new self not born, and ignorant of what these sunrise streaks on my chaos really meant—we had a new kind of meeting in our little community. It was in the old schoolhouse, and because too many came for the seats to hold, we put boards across and filled the aisles, and then brought benches and filled the open space in front, where boys in school time frequently stood as penalty for small offenses. The minister came from a distant town, and bore the distinction of having "elder" before his name. He was a plain, simple, straightforward, good man, who knew a few clear truths of Christianity, and he told them impressively.

At first we boys, who filled a large corner, went for fun, and because we liked to sing the new hymns which he introduced—the Sankey hymns, which were then all fresh from the writer's pen—and "singing in meeting" was a most wonderful innovation. It, however, soon ceased to be "fun," and grew more serious, for I saw that I was approaching an unescapable decision. Each night it became clearer that there were only two kinds of lives—with two distinct issues. What had been dim and vague in my long struggle had suddenly become sharp and clearly defined. I was a poor, sick soul, unable to cure myself, and here the remedy was described. I was drifting hopelessly down the stream. Now I heard what lay at the end of such a course. I knew I wanted something which I had always just missed, now I heard how a life gets completed and saved.

But here I was, a boy among a great group of boys who had followed my lead in a hundred boyish pranks. I could not take a step without breaking a thousand threads which wove my life into the past and bound me up with this society of my fellows. There were days of this seething struggle, during which I felt that my entire future was at stake. At length one night there came a bursting point, and I arose with every artery in me throbbing and my heart pounding so hard that I thought everybody must hear it. With a tremendous effort I made my tongue say, "I want to be a Christian." Nobody laughed; it was still and solemn. I knew I had won my first great spiritual victory. I had made my aspiration "public," in the presence of my old companions. I had believed that the line between the dead self and the new-born being was so sharp and definite that if I had once passed it I should live in perpetual joy, and all struggle would henceforth be over. On the contrary, I do not think any great wave of joy or flood of bliss swept over me. I simply knew I had crossed a line. The more I saw what the goal was, the more I knew I had only made a beginning. The next great battle came some days later, when I felt that I must get down before the whole meeting and pray. I cannot tell to this day whether I was afraid of the people or whether I was awed at the thought of addressing God. I only know that I got down and made my lips go, but not a word came. I seemed paralyzed at the immensity of the undertaking. Everybody saw me, but nobody heard me.

In spite of times of swelling joy, when I knew I had really passed a crisis in the incubation of a new life, I still found that the old self was far from dead, and that I often slipped back into the ways I had left. The new land was in sight, and yet the cables which bound me to the old shores were not entirely cut. But this much must be said, that after that memorable day in the schoolhouse I never had any doubt that God was for me, or any permanent sense that He would let go of me.

CHAPTER X

THE FAITH AND THE LIFE

All through my boyhood I had thought of religion as a means of getting to heaven. The joy and relief which came to me in the moment of my surrender in the old schoolhouse, were saturated with the feeling of a certainty of heaven. I always had had a terror of death, not because I was afraid that my being would be ended by death, but much more because I was afraid of waking up after death in surroundings which were extremely dreadful. I often tried without much success to picture the scenery and circumstances of my soul after it should "cross the river." One of my little playfellows, whose life had surely never set toward goodness, was suddenly stricken down. I saw him laid away in the unattractive little graveyard, but I knew that this did not end his career. I wondered what was happening to him in his new place. How he must want to be alive again to get different before his case was eternally settled! But I knew he never could have another chance.

Now, however, I had the joy of feeling that my soul was saved, that if I died, as I had once come very near doing, I should be in blissful happiness forever. It is impossible for any one who has not had this experience to realize in any degree what it means. There are few moments in one's life which give any joy to compare with it. To be suddenly assured in your own soul that heaven, all you have ever imagined or dreamed of peace and joy, is to be yours, and that the celestial gate will open at your knock when you come to it—this is certainly a supreme experience, and I had the thrill of it.

Men and women who are absorbed in the strenuous work and rush of this busy and material world hardly ever fully realize how seriously children think of heaven, how real a place it is to them. Unseen things are just as real to them as seen things are. The extreme conscientiousness with which some boys and girls are affected, even to a morbid degree, often grows out of their magnified sense of the reality of heaven and hell, and the effect of this upon their fears and hopes. And the deeper this sense of the unseen, the higher will be the joy and peace which sweeps over the soul when it attains an assurance of salvation. This at least is borne out in my boyish experience.

But I soon found, what also I had probably all along dimly and vaguely known, that religion is concerned with something more than getting to heaven. It was this "something more" which made my new experience not altogether a joyous one. In some degree I realized now that I must be every day and in every place and under all sorts and conditions of life a new kind of person. I began to see that there was no immediate prospect of going to heaven, but instead of that an unescapable requirement upon me to be good here in the complex surroundings of this present world.

I now began to be haunted by the idea that I could never really like myself, that is, be satisfied, until I was every bit good, while all the time this attainment seemed an almost hopeless quest. The result was that I had, in this period, moments of wonderful happiness when I thought of the future life, and imagined myself an inhabitant of the heavenly city, followed by other times of depression, when I saw myself as I really was—far from heavenly in nature, and as unangelic as boys usually are. I kept up a vague hope, which I sometimes put into a prayer, that by some miraculous event I might be made good, and so have the struggle done with; that, in a word, I might anticipate heaven, and find out here what it was like to be every whit good and do now the kind of things I should do when I got to be truly an angel.

I think that my Uncle Eli more than anybody else helped me to realize—not by what he said, but by what he did—that this goodness of character which I was after is not something miraculous that drops into a soul out of the skies, but is rather something which is formed within as one faithfully does his set tasks, and goes to work with an enthusiastic passion to help make other people good. I saw him growing white and bent with the advance of years, but no touch of age in the slightest degree weakened his efforts to make our neighborhood better. He preached the gospel on the first day of the week, and the next day worked at a scheme for building up a town library. One day he was trying to do something to destroy the saloon and advance the cause of temperance, and the next he would be raising money to endow an educational institution. Now he would be busy organizing a local missionary society, and the next day he might be advocating a better system of taxation for the town. If he drove by he might be on his way to the station to start off for an extended religious visit, or he might be going down the road to visit a sick neighbor. In all his work for the betterment of man at home and abroad, I never saw him discouraged or in doubt about the final issue. He was always full of hope and courage, and radiantly happy to be able to work at human problems.

But the thing which impresed me most, as a thoughtful boy, was that in all this perplexing and wearying work, he was becoming more and more like my ideal of a saint. His face was sunny; his smile was always ready to break out. We were all happier when he came, and he himself seemed to have a kind of inward peace which was very much like what I supposed the heavenly beings had. It had been his preaching which had so influenced my very early life; but it was much more his victorious life, which spoke with an unanswerable power like that of a sunset or the starry sky, that influenced me now in this critical time. I felt that the way to become good was to go to work in the power of God to help make others good, and to help solve the problems of those among whom we live.

I got a further impression of this truth from an event which came at first as a calamity. I went out one morning in early winter to feed our cattle and horses in the barn, and found to my horror that a fearful storm in the night had blown the barn down with almost everything we possessed in it. It was such a wreck as I had never seen. I can remember now the way I felt as I ran through the neighborhood to call the men together to see if we could save anything. The news went fast, and before the day was over men from near and far gathered in our yard. They were all hard working people like ourselves, with little wealth beyond their own strong hands. But before they separated they had decided to go to work at once and replace what the storm had destroyed. The entire neighborhood went to work, and a new structure rose where the ruin had been.

It was a simple deed, which perhaps many towns could parallel, but it affected me in a strange way. I saw, as I had not seen before, that the religion of these men was not merely an affair of the meeting-house; not merely a way to get to heaven. It was something which made them thoughtful of others and ready to sacrifice for others. I saw how it worked itself out in practical deeds of kindness and righteousness. During those days that I worked in the cold of a Maine winter, among those men with their rough clothes and hard hands, I was helping build more than a barn; I was forming a wider view of the religion which such men as these were living by.

CHAPTER XI

THE GREAT MYSTERY

A boy has many sorrows to bear. It is very much to be questioned whether there is any other decade in the ordinary person's life which has so many periods of grief and sadness as the one which covers that marvelous epoch from five to fifteen. This is, of course, not the generally accepted view of a boy's life. The average is not dark, but bright, and yet the pain spots are very numerous.

The fifteen-year-old boy in the country has tasted almost every kind of hard experience. He can give the moral philosopher, who is in search of wisdom, points on the real balance between pain and happiness. No matter how true and watchful his household may be in their relations to him, he still has many melancholy times, when he feels alone in the universe, with his own inward battles to fight which drive him apart from men, and make his world seem as solitary as Adam's before his companion appeared. He does not in the remotest degree understand himself when he is out of the noisy crowd where he has been playing and shouting as though he had no more burdens or problems than the unweaned lamb.

My associations during this trying period of inward perplexity and mystery were almost entirely with companions who were irreligious, who used all the forms of profanity and vulgarity known to the country youth. It apparently never had any serious influence upon me. I enjoyed their company, liked them, and threw myself into their fun, yet, as I have said, I never used their expressions, and as soon as I was alone again I was in my other world, where only God and myself knew of the spiritual conflict.

It may be inferred that my above stated belief that all boys have their lonely times and their hard periods is based only on my own experience, while the prevailing belief is that most boys are careless and akin to the vegetable in their lack of serious concern. Those who hold that view do not know boys well. They will deceive the most watchful with their unconcern, but the moment they are alone, and are no longer acting a part, they are another order of being. Catch the careless boy unawares and touch his quick with skillful finger, and you will always find that his tears flow extremely easily.

There is one event which can never be repeated in this world, let it come when it will. It stands all alone, and it leaves a touch on one's entire self which all the passing years fail to remove. That is the death of a mother. This came to me while I was still in the stress of this outwardly-smooth, inwardly-rough period, so difficult to describe, so real in experience. I had often wondered whether I should go on living if mother were to die, whether it would be possible to eat and drink, work and sleep, if she were gone. I thought about it because she was extremely frail, and steadily grew more saintly-spiritual and less equal to the burden of the work she wanted to do. I had, however, endless faith that either the doctor would make her better, or that some change would come to make her strong again. It was a great comfort when the visiting ministers prayed for her—that the Lord would raise her up to strength. I felt sure it must be so. No other outcome was really thinkable; and I always ended by believing that we were to live on together just as we always had. A boy's judgment is invariably colored by his wishes.

But on one memorable day all my hopes were shattered. The stroke fell. I had to face the reality. I stood confronted with the most stubborn, inexorable fact. It seemed impossible, and yet there it was. It ought not to be, and yet nothing could change it. I thought of all the cases I had ever read or heard of in which persons had been mistaken in calling some one dead. I clung like a drowning man to the vague hope that it might be a prolonged sleep, and that she would awaken and surprise us all. I strangely felt myself in the great company of sufferers all over the world, as though we belonged in one common fellowship. I saw a boy with whom I had often quarreled go by the house. I thought only of the bare fact that he had lost his mother, and so was in my group, and I burst into tears as I watched him.

Then followed my great rebellion—the worst I have ever known. Could a God be good who took away my mother? Could there be any Heart of Love in a universe where such things happened? I had never had the slightest doubt of an immortal life after this one. I had taken it as though it were as much a settled fact as that the sun which went down in the west at night would come up in the east next morning. Now I felt the ground going out from under this entire faith. My whole structure seemed toppling over. My prayers sounded hollow, and the kindly words of comfort spoken to me were empty words. It seemed at first as though this state of things would last forever. I saw no way out of it. I had come upon a mental condition as new as it was to the first man who ever faced death. Every rope in my ship was tested. The question was being settled, however little I knew it, whether I was to go to wreck or come through the storm with a stauncher faith than I had ever known before.

The issue was determined, not by any one thing, not by any one sharply defined experience, but rather by the trend of my entire previous life. My religion had been forming from babyhood up. It was as much a part of me as the color of my eyes or my sense of space and time. I could not remember a time when I had not loved God and felt sure of His love. I had had my stages of development and of inward contest, but I had been perfectly sure of God all the time. Now my faith was suffering eclipse because I could not square this terrible event with my idea of a God of love.

But little by little the memories of sixteen years came over this dark event with their trail of light. God had given me my mother, and through her I had learned of Him. There were hundreds of bright points in our lives together when her love and patience had helped me to rise to my consciousness of God. I could not forget how I had heard her in her prayers talk quietly with Him about me, as though she knew Him perfectly and wanted to make me acquainted with Him. I knew, too, that she fully expected to go on living with Him after death should come to her. It had apparently never occurred to her that death would do more than separate her from us. My trouble had largely come because I could not get my thoughts above the earth over her coffin.

But as her faith in a new and larger life came over me and quickened my own, and as I settled back on all the sure evidences that all my life had been in the love of God, I began to realize that I had not lost my mother, that she was nearer to God than ever, and that I was more than ever bound to live her kind of life. But I came out of this struggle no longer a child. I had wrestled with an angel in the dark, and when I emerged with the blessing, I had passed a crisis.

With this event came also the uprooting of my life from its old environment. I passed from the education which home and the free country life had to give to the more exact discipline and training of an old, well-established boarding school. I had never before been much beyond the horizon line which I could see from the hill-top in our field. Only once had I wandered as far as twenty miles from our house. Now I discovered a world as new to me as the one which broke upon Columbus' sight when his keel grated on the shores of San Salvador. I shall try to tell in another chapter what that new experience meant, but I cannot forget that my break with the old home and my migration to boarding school mark a dividing line which severs my life into two very diverse epochs. The period of which I have been speaking lies over on the far side of that great division line. I have been talking about the "self" I "remember"; on this side that line it will be a little more clearly the "self" I "am and know."

Here I have given some backward glimpses upon my religious life as it slowly formed. It probably seems more somber than it really was. It has been necessary to touch the deeper moments, to catch the crucial experiences. It may give the impression that I was not the ordinary, rollicking, healthy boy, but a child who lived apart and dwelt excessively on what was going on within. This would be a totally wrong impression and would spoil my story. I was never thought of by the neighbors as a "good boy." They saw in me the incarnation of the country boy—reckless, stormy, fun-loving, a natural product of the lake and the woods, as free as a bird, and as devoid of conscience pricks as an animal. "What *will* he make?" was the frequent query. I have told my inner side because I believe it is not extraordinary, but a somewhat common experience. Boys are much deeper, much better, than even their *mothers* know, and down below what they show and what they say, is a center of life which never is wholly silent. If their friends knew how to reach it there would be more good men in the world than there are!

CHAPTER XII

A NEW EPOCH BEGINS

One memorable day when the evening mail came in there was a letter for me—always a rare event—which brought the momentous news that I had been granted a free scholarship in the famous Friends School in Providence, Rhode Island—now the Moses Brown School. I can still feel the heave of emotion as I read the shining message, and then with winged feet took the word to the assembled family. I was within half a year of seventeen, very thin, nearly six feet tall, extremely green, and awkward, but wide awake, keen, eager, and ambitious. I had never seen a real city. I had never been inside a railroad train. I had no idea what a steamboat was like, nor could I imagine what a horse-car could be like, running on a city street. I went to Boston on the steamboat, "Star of the East," and then to Lynn, Massachusetts, where two of my Hoxie Aunts lived, and after a brief visit in a world unlike any I had seen, I went to Providence by train and found a horse-car which took me to the school on the hilltop, overlooking the long expanse of

Narragansett Bay. I felt very far from home and thoroughly uncomfortable.

I was deeply impressed by the grandeur of the place, however, the immense buildings with high ceilings, extensive grounds beautifully kept, and the splendid vistas out into a world of novelty and wonder. There were one hundred and twenty-five boys and the same number of girls. Among them were some of the finest persons I have ever known, but that fact was not in evidence that sad first day. I missed the old scenes, I longed for the old surroundings and companions and I did not know how to adjust to conditions and circumstances so absolutely unfamiliar. I dreaded the dining-room most, with unknown girls in front of me and unknown boys on each side of me. I dreaded reciting in classes where everybody was a stranger and I dreaded sleeping in a room with a boy whose name I hardly knew. My roommate was the first person I had ever seen kneel down and pray before going to bed. I always prayed, but I did it in quiet and silence after getting into bed. It must have taken some courage for my bedfellow, who certainly was not a saint, to carry through his habit of prayer that first night and to give me my first lesson. The strangeness and the dread soon passed. I made friends rapidly and soon had my intimate circle. I found five cousins in the school whom I had never seen before. I was strong and physically powerful and I was in demand on the athletic teams. As soon as I began to find myself I became less awkward and self-conscious.

In the classroom I quickly came to the fore. It might naturally be supposed that my years in country school, with no teacher who had ever been to college, would have left me far behind the boys of my own age. But that was not the case. I was perfectly at home in arithmetic and algebra and had gained somewhat unusual mathematical insight and accuracy. I had spent three months, the year before, at Oak Grove Seminary, where I began Latin with a college graduate, so that I was able now to start with the Caesar class and to maintain its pace. My home school had no doubt lacked many things. It had almost no science and it failed to correct some of our faults in grammar and pronounciation, but it had nevertheless, laid for me a good foundation for my future intellectual structure. I had not been taught to write essays and I had no skill at all in literary composition, but I had learned to speak in public with considerable ease and I could face an audience and "declaim" with some degree of abandon and enthusiasm. I had acquired a passion for study and I had gained an intellectual interest—an immense asset at seventeen—and I now forged forward by leaps and bounds.

It was soon settled that I could graduate from the school in two years, which brought me into the largest, and perhaps the most distinguished, graduating class which the school up to that time had ever had. There were twenty-five of us, ten boys and fifteen girls. With members of this group I formed friendships which were to know no end and received influences which were precious beyond calculation. What is there that can compare with these intimate fellowships in school? Life's burdens have not arrived yet, cares and problems are not heavy, or at least they are not enduring. There is a superfluous energy of youth which makes living a joy and this community life with congenial spirits adds the last touch to a perfect stage of being. I cannot be too thankful for my friendships with some of the finest girls in the class and in the school. Coeducation in boarding schools seems to be passing by, and where it is not being given up, it is under debate. I know from much experience the difficulties involved in it and even in our early, simpler time there was much to criticize, but the refining influence of the association in classes and at table was an important factor in my education, while the sincere and unaffected friendship of girls who had nobility of character, grace of manner, and purity of spirit raised me to a new level of life. In these matters there is safety in numbers, and I rejoice that at this stage I did not concentrate my attention on one, but formed a happy and lasting friendship with many. Foolish and frivolous talk with girls of my own age had been a common enough experience in my home period, but now I learned the art of conversation, the interchange of thought, the give and take of ideas, the discussion of books and events, and with these things the added pleasure which comes from the charm of personality and the beauty of face and character.

I had a remarkable group of teachers here whose touch and influence upon my life were potent factors in the formation of it. I was far more advanced in mathematics than in any other branch, and in this field I now had excellent teaching and inspiring leadership. I have never enjoyed any mental work more than I did my geometry, trigonometry and surveying. The classroom work, the illuminating talks of my teacher, John Myron Potter, the challenging rivalry of brilliant fellow-students and the slow and patient solution of problems out of class awakened my mind and called forth my latent powers. The bearing of all this on my religious life no doubt seems remote, but nothing that quickens the mind and forms the inner life is unimportant. Religion is not something foreign, not something superadded to the fundamental nature of the soul. It has to do rather with the whole process of self-development and with the building of those ideals by which we live.

My study of Latin and Greek proved to be one of the greatest formative forces of my entire life. Through these two languages and literatures I came into intimate first hand contact with the culture of two of the greatest civilizations of human history. The mastery of a language in itself is a unique source of intellectual power. Then the language when it is mastered at once becomes a means and instrument for the accumulation of facts and knowledge. Furthermore, no one ever truly knows a great piece of literature unless he reads it in the language in which the author of it first wrote it. That is true even of all great prose, but it is supremely true of poetry. I felt this first with my Virgil, then with Horace, and, in a much greater degree, with Homer, all of whom I read quite extensively in the school period.

One of the great permanent assets from my work with the classics was the effect of it on my English style. My teacher, Seth K. Gifford, was a sound classical scholar and he insisted on a mastery of the declension of nouns, the conjugation of verbs, including all of the irregular ones, and the rules of grammar. But not less important was his rigid requirement of a careful, accurate rendering of every passage into good English. No "good enough" translation would ever pass. It had to be *right*. He made us work on it until the great passage of the Latin or Greek author came over into English that fitted it. I had never been able to write with any ease at all. My letters were wooden, my essays were crude and flat. But here in these classes I began to feel the majestic power and beauty of language, the charm and elegance of style, the importance of the *way* in which a thing is expressed. There may be other forms of intellectual culture which do as much toward unfolding of *capacities* and the formation of the mental life, but I have never found anything which seems to me can compare with the classics.

Much more direct in its influence on my religious thought was my work in science with the veteran science teacher, Thomas J. Battey. He had a noble veneration for truth, a rare power of observation, a passion for accuracy—all important traits in science—and with these qualities he had an almost unlimited joy in nature and enthusiasm for search and discovery. He soon made me one of his companions. We walked the woods and fields together. He showed an almost miraculous power of vision and hearing. He would see a rare flower that escaped every other eye. He would hear an insect which all the rest of us missed. He awakened our interest in the most common objects. I remember hearing him say, "I would rather know the history of every stone in that wall than to have a million dollars." Of course, he would! Every clay bank, with its lines of erosion, interested him as much as a gold mine, or an oil deposit, would have done. This dear man—a born poet and a great Christian as well as a scientist—taught me geology. I first heard in his classes the astonishing fact that the world was not made in six days, six thousand odd years ago, but had a history of uncounted and uncountable years. He marshalled the evidence. He made the *fact* as clear and plain as morning sunrise. He laid before us the marvelous story of the evolution of the horse. He showed us the array of fossils. He pointed out how the stages of the embryo child run in a parallel order to the stages of the order of evolving life. Most important of all he carried us over from our childish idea of a God who worked from the outside like a mechanic to the higher conception of a God who works from within as a living creative energy. He helped us to realize that the account in Genesis is a great poetic story through which some man in the primitive stages of human thought expressed the central truth of the ages that God is the Maker of all that is. This account, he made us feel, is not in terms of science, which was not born yet, but in terms of poetry and art and religion, which are as old as smiling and weeping. This beautiful sweep of inspired vision, he convinced us, offers no bar or hindrance to exact research and is not a substitute for a careful, reasoned, demonstrable method of divine creation. What all this meant to me, with my previous insular outlook and child-minded conceptions, can hardly be expressed. In any case, I leaped forward to the new view and with it I won my spiritual freedom. I had grasped an Ariadne thread which was to be a constant and never failing clue. My college studies and my reading of Henry Drummond a little later were to take me into regions into which I had not yet travelled; but Thomas Battey put the key into my hand which unlocked many doors, and he helped me to pass from a child's religion to that of a robust developing youth, and enabled me to cross this important bridge without any wreckage of faith.

In this period was also born my love of literature. I studied English Literature with Henry Wood, later a distinguished professor in Johns Hopkins University. He was the first person I had ever seen who had a Ph.D. after his name. He not only took me through the long line of great English writers and reviewed their biographical history, but he also had us read and study some of the most famous poems of the greatest poets, beginning with Chaucer's *Canterbury Tales.* With him also I studied what used to be called "Mental Philosophy." It was my introduction to the problems to which I have since devoted a large part of my life. The book we used was dry and abstruse, but the teacher was a live man, and he opened up many questions which touched the central realities of the soul and the universe. During my last important year in the school—a postgraduate year to complete my preparation in Greek—I was thrown intimately with Dr. Benjamin Wells, who introduced me to Lowell's "Biglow Papers," which gave me immense delight. This rich Yankee humor exactly fitted my nature and spirit. From "Biglow Papers" I went on into Lowell's more serious poems—especially "The Commemoration Ode" and "The Cathedral," and for the next period of my life Lowell was my greatest loved poet, my constant inspiration. I knew by heart long passages of his best poems and I owe to him much of my moral passion and my deeper religious faith. I also owe to him my first awakening of interest in American History. It was at this period that there was born within me, never to die, an intense feeling of patriotism for *the country that ought to be, for an ideal America.* "Biglow Papers," "Present

Crisis," "Commemoration Ode," and other poems on national issues, sent me to books on our historical and political life. Charles Sumner and John Quincy Adams became at this time my two foremost heroes. I learned their speeches by heart and declaimed them, I read their biographies and thrilled over their battles for the freedom of the slave. It was many years later before Lincoln rose to first place in my list of American heroes. It is odd that this should have been so, but so it was.

Our school meeting, which was held on Sunday and Wednesday mornings, was a Quaker Meeting conducted in the main after the ancient Quaker fashion, that is with considerable silence and no singing, though we were certain to have a short sermon from Allen Jay, who was at this period an officer of the school. This remarkable man, from the middle West, was a good spiritual guide for young people. He told striking anecdotes, was rich in illustration, put his message into the concrete and held our interest and attention, and what was better, had our affection. He was strongly evangelical, but it was always religion of experience, not theory and theology, which he gave us. We had our own evening prayer-meetings which we ourselves "led' in turn, and this responsibility gave me my first practical experience in the conduct of a meeting and in addressing others on religious topics. It was all crude, no doubt, but those first trembling steps on the right path led on to more. My beloved cousin, Augustine Jones, was head-master of the school and he taught our Bible Class on Sunday. It was a new type of Bible teaching, broad, intelligent, full of practical experience and well illustrated with the fruit of reading and travel. His advice, his constant friendship with me, his encouragement and spiritual leadership through these years are blessings never to be forgotten.

The Quaker Meeting in Providence at this time was a conservative one. The old ways and the old ideals still held sway there. I did not often "go down town" to meeting, but I met some of the city Friends and received a certain touch of influence from them. I had already begun to watch with keen interest the conflict between the ancient type of Quakerism and what was called then the "progressive" type. My sympathies were with the staid, quiet, seasoned form of worship, with hush and silence as the basis, rather than with the oncoming innovations. It was in the dull old meeting house on Main Street that some of the early "battles" of this conflict were waged. The Newport and Portsmouth Friends tended to be "progressive," and those who moved in this direction looked upon the Providence Friends as very "conservative" and as a brake on the car of progress. One famous day, when Rhode Island "Quarterly Meeting" was being held in Providence, some of the "progressives" from the south end of the state came up in force to "wake up" the quiet northern section which seemed to them in a Rip Van Winkle sleep. The innovators used all the tactics known to "progressives." They sang a hymn after an ancient Friend had exhorted the meeting to "gather into the silence of all flesh." They prayed long prayers in standing posture, then a great innovation. They said "amen" to one another's testimonies, also a great innovation. At length, when the new ways had reached their climax, an aged Friend of much experience in the interior life rose with great dignity and said, "When I listen to the noisy efforts of this misguided people, I feel to say with the prophet Elijah, 'call Him louder, peradventure He sleepeth!'" Her voice was rhythmic and quavery with emotion, and the scene was very humorous, but nobody laughed. It called the meeting back to reverence and to quiet. My cousin Charles and I *felt amen* for the remarks of the ancient speaker.

I have spoken in a general way of the delightful fellowship which I had with my classmates and others in the school, but I should like to single out three persons from the group for a few sacred words of loving memory. Their lives are forever closely intertwined with mine. Charles R. Jacob was a second cousin of mine and a companion, as I have previously said, from early childhood. The friendship between us was a steadily growing one. He was much more precocious than I was; in advance of me in most things and far more refined in manner and taste. He had a genuine poetic gift and had written good verses from his earliest youth. He had remarkable humor, though his shyness and modesty kept him from letting go and revealing himself. We became united in deep affection and death has only intensified my love for this rare soul. Alice Jones was a distant cousin whom I had never seen before our school life brought us together in the same class. She had an angelic face, and might well have sat for one of Sir Joshua Reynolds' angels. Something of the world she was soon to inhabit was already radiant in her form and features. She was extraordinarily pure and devout, but she had nevertheless a good fund of humor and was full of life and spirit. She was one of the first of our group to go into the larger light and life, but she did not go until something of her spirit had been laid upon me. Edward L. Farr has only recently, in 1924, broken his visible relations with me. It was only slowly at school that the web of our friendship was woven. We were very unlike in disposition and interests, but we were thrown together in classes, in work and in daily contacts, and a fire of affection was kindled in our hearts, never to go out. For over forty years we grew steadily nearer and dearer to one another. Years might go by without a meeting, but it made no difference. Our paths in life diverged widely, but one understood the other as perfectly as though we had everything in common. There is no way of telling what those three friends of my youth—all now in the light that has no shadows—have added of joy and love to my journey of life.

This story of those wonderful years is not in true perspective. A few peaks of memory stand out here, but the everyday plain from which the peaks rose is only dimly projected. There was much serious work, but there was also much sport, rare fun, high spirits and very little care and worry. Once when the school was passing through an epidemic of scarlet fever from which one of our students died, I was taken ill and reported by the nurse to be a victim of the dreaded disease. I was isolated in a remote room in the spooky upper regions of the main building, where I passed an anxious day, alone with a Bible, expectant of an early death. But at the end of the seemingly interminable day it was decided that I showed no signs of the scarlet pestilence and I once more joined the human throng below—a happy boy that night!

My religious life at this stage was steadily developing. I was always reckoned among the religious boys of the school and I wanted to be counted as such. I was, however, in no narrow sense "pious" or "other worldly." I was in everything that happened, full of life, eager for adventure and ready to have my share in all affairs that were going forward. Nevertheless, I had a religious background and a strong moral fiber. There were well-formed ideals in my soul, which drew me on and which held like adamant whenever a crisis came. My religion during this period was not so strongly inward and mystical as it had been in early home days. I was now bringing forward the historical and objective side of my faith. I was living in a world of facts and events, and discovering the way in which Christianity had shaped and organized the course of history and the progress of the centuries. I was interested in moral crises and the contribution of heroic souls. This was all to the good and was building up a greatly needed strand of my spiritual life. College was to send me back again to the mystical side of life and to cultivate the interior strand of my faith and it was well to have the balance preserved and maintained. It was a time of splendid health and vitality and I grew more steady and normal each year. My numerous friends, with a great variety of traits and manners, helped tremendously to organize my life and to draw out my developing powers. I found myself being believed in and trusted. I could not fail to see that I had the confidence and respect of students and teachers. This never in the least gave me a sense of pride or conceit, but it rather touched me with wonder and humility. I could not understand it and I never have understood it. I only know that other people's faith in you works almost like a miracle in your career and mission. It is very odd how we go on and progress steadily forward without seeing the way onward and without knowing clearly whither we are going. I had only the dimmest notion of what I was going to be or of what I *wanted* to be. I only knew vaguely that I was going on. I was in the condition of the wild geese whom I had so often watched migrate. They kept a fixed *direction* but they did not know where their terminus was to be. I myself often used to go home from the village store when the night was pitch dark, black as polar midnight. I could not see an inch ahead. Not a sign furnished a clue of the homeward way. But my feet always felt the road underneath and kept me going on toward the hidden goal, until I finally caught a glimpse of mother's light near the window. Life has a good deal of the time been like that, and especially so in these years at school, but I was favored with a sense of direction and God's hand was surely guiding, even when I hardly touched it.

This brings me to another great divide. When I left school for college I was no longer a boy. I had a Prince Albert coat! and there were still surer signs that I had overpassed the stage of boyhood. Man perhaps I was not yet, but I was soon to be one and I had already outgrown the ways of the boy, who had "travelled farther from the East." The later story belongs in another book. I hope some day it will get told, for there are no more important epics than those of the inner life. If a man can succeed in telling about the building of his soul, it is more worth while than the telling of any other kind of tale.